THE OTHER CHEEK

THE OTHER CHEEK

*gospel, empire, and memory
in one Christian's journey*

CORDELL STRUG

WIPF & STOCK · Eugene, Oregon

To the Peacemakers of the Christian Community

Wipf and Stock Publishers
199 W 8th Ave, Suite 3
Eugene, OR 97401

The Other Cheek
Gospel, Empire, and Memory in One Christian's Journey
By Strug, Cordell
Copyright©2018 by Strug, Cordell
ISBN 13: 978-1-5326-8845-4
Publication date 4/12/2019
Previously published by Ytterli Press, 2018

CONTENTS

I. JOURNEY /1

II. WAR /37
    Church Newsletter, October 2002
    Iraq War, March, 2003

III. MEMORY /53
    2003
    2004
    2007
    2008
    2009

IV. JUDGMENT /107

You have heard that it was said, "An eye for an eye and a tooth for a tooth." But I say to you, Do not resist an evildoer. But if anyone strikes you on the right cheek, turn the other also.

—Matthew 5:38–39

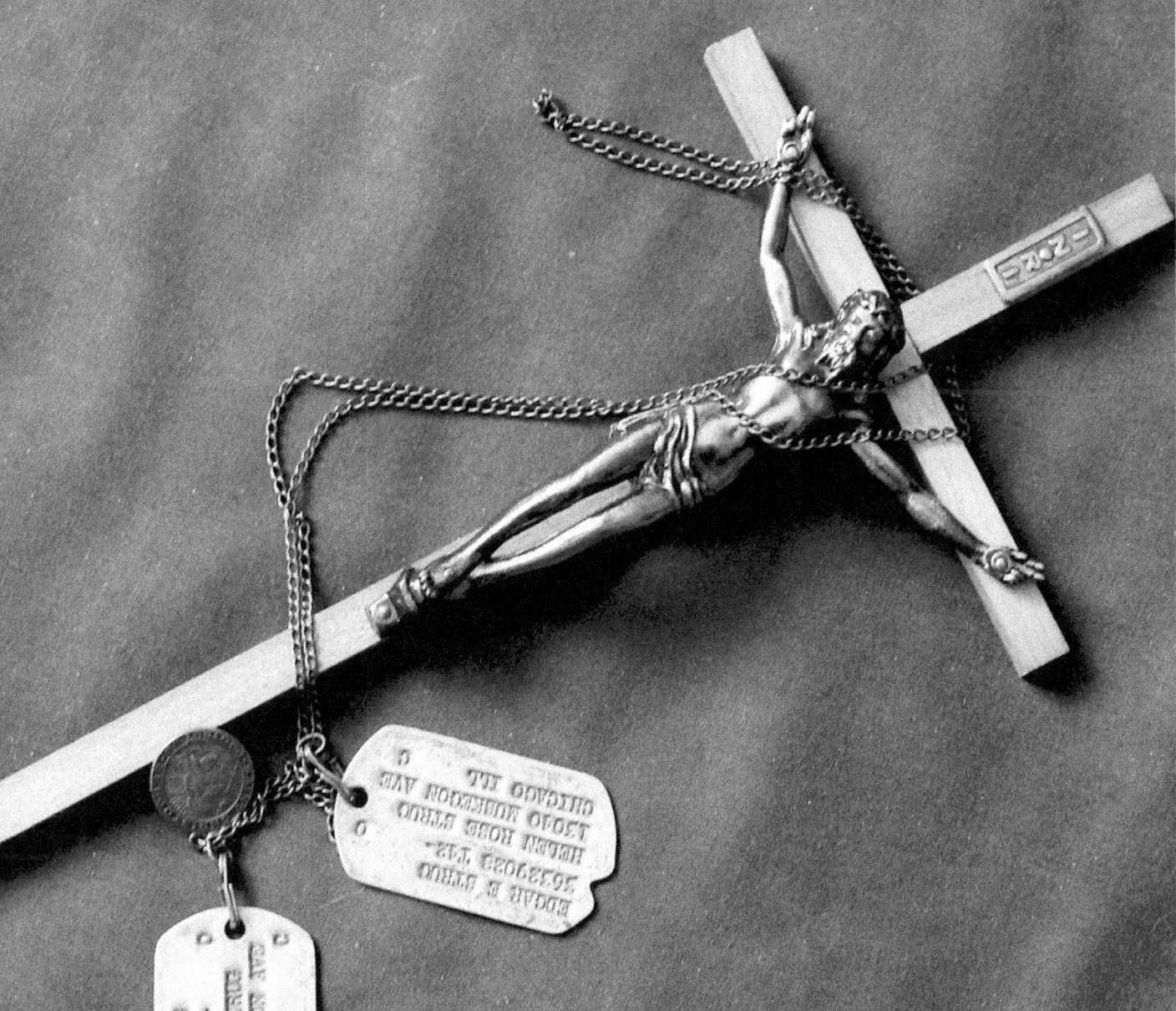

I. JOURNEY

The country has once for all regurgitated the Declaration of Independence and the Farewell Address, and it won't swallow again immediately what it is so happy to have vomited up....It has deliberately pushed itself into the circle of international hatreds, and joined the common pack of wolves....We are objects of fear to other lands.

> —William James, "Address on the Philippine Question," *Proceedings of the Fifth Annual Meeting of the New England Anti-Imperialist League,* December, 1903

I

I have a vivid memory which I think of as my first consciously patriotic encounter. It strikes me as revealing that it's colored by wounded feelings and desperation.

I'm standing by our kitchen sink and my mother is looking down at me. She's jabbing her finger at me to emphasize her points, a gesture I realize I've copied and used my entire life. She speaks in the hard, choppy English she only began learning when she was eleven years old. (It must have sounded that way to ears used to the soft, slushy sounds of Polish.) She says, "If anyone asks you what you are, you tell them you're American. You were born here and you belong here. You just tell them you're as American as they are."

I'm guessing someone must have called me a dumb polack, which sent me running home in tears, hoping to be told exactly what she was telling me.

I was intensely aware that my family had only recently joined the American story. My grandparents all spoke with thick accents. My father's father was almost incomprehensible to me. My mother's mother eventually gave up on English entirely; one of her bilingual children was always around to serve as her interpreter. Like so many children of immigrants, I wanted to escape that strange world of foreign echoes. I would have given anything to have had a name like Adams or Franklin. When ignorant thugs called Poles dirty and dumb, a hurt and hidden part of me wished I could be on their side.

Now, nearing the end of my life, once I open my mouth, no one in the world would take me for anything but an American. But I sometimes find it hard to recognize the country I was so desperate to belong to. I would never have dreamed I would come to think of it as a paranoid empire, a danger to the world and its own worst enemy.

My fear now is that I'll be taken for one of the thugs. I fear that, by my willing ignorance, I'll deserve to be.

II

I served as a small-town Lutheran pastor in Minnesota from 1982 to 2010. Thus, the last decade of my service fell at the beginning of the third Christian millennium, during the increasingly pointless and seemingly endless wars America was fighting in Afghanistan and Iraq.

By then, the Christian faith and war were old friends. By then, America—with its obsessive security and secrecy, universal spying and continual warfare; with its worldwide network of military bases, with the world itself divided into American Military "Commands"—was more than well along in its journey from republic to empire.

I was part of the society that carried on its "business as usual," in that bitter phrase from the time of the Vietnam War, the pointless and seemingly endless war of my youth. But I was a part of that society that spoke, that had a voice, a platform. I had, quite literally, a pulpit.

I might say I wasn't called to analyze, let alone denounce, American society or its government, week by week, but to proclaim the gift and task of the gospel within that society. Still, I certainly didn't avoid social and political issues; one Fourth of July visitor remarked he was shocked at how political my sermon was. But, looking back, I think it was American greed and bigotry that drew my words and thoughts more often than our military adventures or the decay of democracy.

But there was one time that forced a confrontation with the fact and the force of war: Memorial Day Weekend, especially in the years when the Iraq war was going sour. I thought it might be of some historical interest to gather up a number of the sermons I gave on the Sunday of that weekend over the years, to see what a person like me, with the calling I had, found to say about war and peace in that time.

These sermons could, no doubt, provide nothing but more evidence of how powerful an idol a nation can be and how timid a Christian can be before it.

But first I want to call up some moments from my own journey to that time.

III

In an early memory of my father, I am standing, again, at our kitchen sink. I am older now and I must have just said something naively idealistic and noble, something about America, either to display my nobility or to see what he thought.

He doesn't seem to regard what I've said as a subject for serious discussion, let alone affirmation. He looks out the window and says, "You're going to find out this country isn't as free as you think it is."

I don't remember replying. His unexpected declaration must have had an impact because it's a moment that has risen often to my mind, and I've tried to puzzle out what was behind his words. There was a time I thought he must have been disgusted with the McCarthy witch hunt, simply because I was disgusted when I read of it a few years later. But he never said, I never asked him, and, as our politics drifted apart, the time had passed.

I have heard many people say similar things. They might be angry, bitter, cynical, rueful, hopeless. They might be so convinced of the obvious truth of what they're saying that they say it as a joke and expect to get a laugh. The words by themselves can mean almost anything.

But I remember that I took them, rightly or not, as a warning and a summons to think.

IV

My first memory that has to do with the Second World War is of my father sitting on the edge of my bed and obsessively reliving his part in it. His war stories were my bedtime stories.

I don't have a single sharp memory of this ritual; I see him sitting there, staring away from me into the room, night after night, talking about the war. I thought, childishly, he was generously giving me his time, entertaining me with stories that were more thrilling than those on television because they were real and the man on my bed was in them. It never occurred to me that I had little to do with his presence there or that his need might be greater than mine.

This was one of the constants of my childhood, and I can't remember when it stopped. I suppose, by the time it did, the presence of those moments in my life was so fixed they would never leave me. In fact, the night I remember most clearly was the night my father's father died, and he didn't appear in my bedroom. I remember asking my mother why I couldn't have my story.

I must have been clothing those moments with my own fantasies of heroism and adventure, because the few stories I remember are about fear and pointless loss: being so afraid of drowning that he never wanted to leave the deck of his troop ship in the North Atlantic; lying in terror at night after thinking an unexploded bomb had landed near his foxhole and finding at dawn it was a young pilot whose parachute hadn't opened; being too close to a bombing (which I later realized must have been the carpet bombing of St. Lô) and being shocked by the force of the explosions; shooting a beautiful dog, itself mad with terror, that attacked him in a house he'd entered; almost shooting one of his best friends, who fell into his foxhole during a night alarm. I remember him imitating his friend's scream of terror. I remember thinking it was funny.

My mother, too, would tell stories of when he first returned from the war: she laughed about how he would jump at noises in the street. We lived on the extreme southeast side of Chicago and, at that time, there was still a little hunting that went on there. The story of hers I remember most vividly is of the first day of hunting season his first autumn back: when the guns went off, he leaped from the bed to the floor and started shouting commands. She, too, found such things funny. Neither one of us could imagine what a person who was physically whole, unwounded to our eyes, might be carrying within.

Years later, when I worked for a time in Purdue University's physical plant, there was someone just back from Vietnam who was hired in our shop. He mentioned his service one day and one of the younger men asked him how many people he'd shot. He very slowly put down his tools and lifted his head. He was staring through everything around him, seeing something beyond all of us. Then he turned and walked out of the room.

But that distant stare of his rocked my memory. I had seen it before, many years ago, when I was very small.

V

But to my small self my father was an uncomplicated hero, one of the ordinary heroes that America produced effortlessly, as it produced wheat and steel. I assumed fighting in a righteous cause would leave you untroubled. I thought the only emotions you would feel were pride and satisfaction at a job well done. I remember pitying the children of men who hadn't served, as well as the men themselves. I saw them as sad,

unfulfilled people, silly, useless; I thought of them as slinking about, trying not to be noticed because of their shame.

My father was a sergeant in the Seventh Corps of the First Army who landed in Normandy a few days after D-Day. When I began reading obsessively about World War II, I realized I'd been hearing about the Normandy invasion, the Hurtgen Forest, the Battle of the Bulge, the Nazi party and the death camps for most of my life.

But I absorbed more than the war itself. It's hard to convey now the overwhelming power and unquestionable goodness someone growing up as I did saw in America. We were the free people, those who sacrificed so others might be free. When I was in high school, I remember telling someone I wasn't sure if I should go to college or enlist in the army. In fact, the conversation I recall was more specific than that and revealed my continuing fascination with war: I said I wondered if I should enlist in the army *so I could pilot a helicopter*—that dazzling tactical innovation—*in Vietnam*.

What I ended up doing was going to college, through academic inertia, if nothing else. What I ended up, at last, doing about the war was asking my draft board to classify me as a Conscientious Objector: when they refused and I was drafted, I refused to go and was arrested by the FBI.

I turned away from the only war I was ever offered.

VI

About a year after I retired, I was sitting in a church discussion group that was studying theology in the early church. The pacifism of the early Christians came up and the presider, another retired pastor, about ten years older than I was, looked around the room, judged the age of the group, and said, "Most of the men here must have been in the armed forces. Let's go around the table and say a little bit about where and when we served." There was one younger man who was never faced with the issue, since the draft was gone before he left school, but everyone else had served at one time or another. I don't remember anyone speaking of serious combat, but that doesn't necessarily mean no one saw any.

When my turn came, I said, "Um...well—I was actually arrested by the FBI during the Vietnam war for refusing the draft."

The presider's head jumped a little and he shifted toward me in his seat. "There must be a story there. How did you come to that?"

I find it revealing about the state of the church that none of the veterans were asked how they came, as Christians, to accept the call to military service; that we all assumed it was the pacifist who must provide an explanation. I'll add that this reflection only occurs to me as I write. At the time, I found it unsurprising to be considered the oddity.

But I hadn't really expected to be faced with this issue, and I was no longer used to being put on the spot. So I stuttered a bit, and I might even have turned a little red from finding myself on the spot, but I finally tapped the Bible I'd brought and said something like, "I guess—it was this book. I couldn't get away from stuff like the Sermon on the Mount, that radical nonviolence. I remember feeling...accused by it. By him, by Jesus Christ. It was just something...I guess I would have felt sick, like I'd betrayed something, if I didn't stand up and say I wouldn't go to war." Or something like that.

I do think it's the warriors, not the pacifists, who should be explaining themselves to the Christians. Still, it never occurred to me that night to throw this judgment at the group. I knew as well as they did that I really was the oddity, at least among the Lutherans I served and lived with and the Roman Catholics I'd grown up with; that pacifism really was something I had to make my way to.

So I spent a couple of days thinking again about my path toward making that stand.

The next Sunday, I ran into the class leader during the coffee hour, and we picked up the conversation. I told him I thought the crucial thing forming my experience was the Christian community I was part of at the time. I went to a Methodist college where I majored in philosophy and religion. Some of my teachers were Methodist ministers who very much embodied the social crusading side of Methodism.

It says a great deal about the college that entering freshmen were sent a short reading list, the summer before they arrived, that contained Dietrich Bonhoeffer's *Letters and Papers from Prison*, Kafka's *The Trial*, and Robert Bolt's play *A Man for All Seasons*, works skeptical and defiant of authority, showcasing in Bonhoeffer and Thomas More prisoners of conscience who stood up to the state, one of them during the war my father fought in.

This was in 1964, and the late sixties bore both the idealism of the Civil Rights movement and the pressure of the escalating Vietnam War.

There was an intense student Christian community that formed around the Philosophy and Religion department. It included, as well, the campus liberals attracted by the social conscience awakening there. That community made pacifism a defining mark of serious Christian faith. You felt pushed, always, toward that issue, that decision.

As I was telling this to the class leader, he was nodding. He said, "My community did not make peace an issue." He didn't say it argumentatively or ruefully: it was just so.

"And we really don't make it one now," I said.

"No," he agreed. "We don't."

I remembered how we students had all kept each other brooding on the war. We were set to make it an issue for everyone. I remember going out to the offices of the town's pastors, confronting them about the war, asking how much they were preaching about it, what they were doing to stop it. (One Methodist pastor handed me copies of the sermons he had preached against it.)

When I served in the parish, no one ever walked into my office to find out what I thought about America's wars or even to ask me how a Christian should think about them.

VII

After I applied for Conscientious Objector status, I had a meeting with my draft board. They asked me if I wanted to add anything to the material I had submitted. I said I didn't. They told me I could go. I think it remains the shortest meeting I've ever attended in my life.

They turned me down.

The day I was ordered to report to the Induction Center in Chicago, I carried with me a letter stating that I would refuse induction because I felt strongly I deserved to be classified as a C.O. on religious grounds. I was following a kind of outline prepared by the American Friends Service Committee. (The Committee did outstanding work: they told you what to expect, they told you what you could do and how to do it, they helped you find a lawyer.) It never occurred to me to do anything but make a formal refusal and take whatever happened. I kept thinking about Socrates after his trial, refusing to leave Athens, drinking the hemlock.

Still, when I walked up the street from the commuter station toward the Induction Center, I wasn't really sure what would happen after I presented my letter or where I'd be at the end of the day. The building looked pretty grim, and I felt pretty small, pretty lonely. But once you're settled in yourself, it's easier to keep going than to do anything else.

I walked through the doors and saw a corporal at the top of the stairs, directing everyone. He looked younger than I was. I told him, as the AFSC had instructed, that I wanted to see the officer in charge.

He opened his mouth, frowned, and said, "Right now, I think that's me."

I handed him my letter. His frown deepened. I knew I was ruining his day. He read it, refolded it, and handed it back. He leaned toward me and whispered, "Look: the first thing you're going to do is take the physical. A lot of people fail it. Go through it—if you fail, go home and forget about it. If not, you can decide what to do with that later."

I was disappointed that I couldn't get things settled immediately and was even less sure how the day would go. But I appreciated his gesture.

I suppose, by the time I was drafted, the Army had enough experience with people like me to develop its own procedures for moving things along. I was the beneficiary of this, as I was later of the tidy legal formalities I went through at the end of the day. They gave me cause to be thankful for the rituals of civilization.

After I passed the physical, I finally encountered the commanding officer, another affable young man, indifferent to my passions. He had a calendar in his office, counting down the days until his service would end. He would be on his way soon to grad school at, of all places, Purdue University, where I was currently a grad student in philosophy. We had a good time talking about college.

They set up a little room where I could formally refuse to take the single physical step forward that would put me in the army. (The AFSC was vividly blunt about this moment: before the step, you're subject to justice; after the step, you're subject to *military* justice.)

Then he told me I could roam about the building, as long as I didn't leave it. He'd call the FBI and they'd come for me. He offered me a free lunch in the cafeteria, which I felt too sick to eat.

I waited for hours, on my own. I was sitting in some sort of main waiting room when I saw two men in suits and sunglasses walk in. It was the most amusing moment of my day. I thought: it's just like the movies; they really do stick out.

They moved quickly, as though they were in hot pursuit, and ordered me to stand against the wall. I pointed out I was freely surrendering to them and had been waiting for them all day. They searched me for weapons, then, even more absurdly, handcuffed me.

We rode downtown to the Federal Building. I remember glimpsing Chicago's Picasso sculpture.

I had to stand in a cage inside the elevator as we rode upstairs. I wondered what they did with dangerous people until we passed a black prisoner shuffling along with chains around his waist and ankles.

I was photographed, front and profile, and fingerprinted. The man taking my prints said he appreciated how cool younger felons like me were. He hated working with the older, white-collar crooks: their hands were always sweaty and blurred the prints.

There was a brief hearing to set a date for a more formal hearing when my lawyer could be present. The judge said he'd release me on my own recognizance. He told me I was free to go. I was too stunned to marvel at how easy it all had been.

I left the Federal Building, figured out where I was, walked down to the Randolph Street station and took the South Shore train back to my parents' house, where my wife, daughter, mother, and father were waiting to see what would happen to me.

If you're indicted for a federal crime, you're not allowed to leave the district you were indicted in without permission of the court. At my hearing, later that week, I asked for, and easily received, permission to keep attending school in West Lafayette, Indiana. Since I couldn't, without further permission, legally travel anywhere else, even in the United States, that was my world for the next few years.

Then, one day, my case was simply dismissed. Sometime while I was writing my dissertation, I received a copy of the letter the U.S. Attorney sent to my draft board. He pointed out that the religious reasons for my appeal were so clear and so well supported by letters from several Christian ministers that it would have been impossible to convict me. He strongly suggested they stop wasting his time on cases he couldn't win and give me the classification I deserved. They never did give me C.O. status. They simply forgot about me, as I did them. It no doubt helped that I wasn't a very actively troublesome person.

I should fully acknowledge, as well, that in my tiny confrontation with one of the Powers of the Earth, I was always treated pretty gently and my eventual success came by courtesy of that Power's granting exemption from military service to any believer with a troubled conscience. As earthly idols go, the United States of America can sometimes be difficult to scorn absolutely.

VIII

I wasn't much of a radical or a rebel. As I waited for my legal status to clarify, I mostly wanted to continue studying philosophy in peace. The fact of my draft protest and, even more, the fact of my arrest by the FBI became a kind of shield for me, not unlike Henry Fleming's Red Badge of Courage (which he received, you might recall, from being clubbed by another fleeing soldier after he'd fled his first battle). I was spared being asked why I wasn't doing more to stop the war.

I was a mere spectator at the largest anti-war demonstration I ever saw. I turned a corner one morning walking to my office on campus and saw a long line of police officers in riot gear. Up ahead of them was a pretty good-sized crowd, sitting on the pavement, completely blocking the main intersection of the business district.

I believe it was a nationally organized event: "stop business as usual." It was an embodied accusation against American society, for complacently carrying on with its life, business as usual, while the Vietnam War ground on pointlessly, the numbers of the dead and maimed rose and rose, and it seemed both unwinnable and unstoppable. The event was fueled by desperation both simple and moral: many there simply didn't want their loved ones to die, or to die themselves; many were revolted by the slaughter and destruction without reason.

I watched for a time, listened to the speakers, who gave the crowd something to occupy it, then walked on. I think they sat there most of the day. They could have sat there a week and still made little difference.

But that would never have happened either. It wasn't only the business community that wanted to get back to business as usual. Almost everybody, almost always, wants to get back to business as usual. You have to eat, you have to sleep, you have to relieve yourself, you have to find shelter, *you have to provide for your life or have someone do it for you.*

There is a relentlessness to daily life and its tasks because there's a relentless to human need: food, shelter, clothing. And, beyond the need, there is the sheer variety and boundlessness of human desire, the wish to seek out your own satisfaction, to go on with your own life in your own way.

I reflected later that the only thing that could have kept a crowd that size in place (or kept it coming back) for long enough to make a difference was the kind of authoritarian force, discipline, and supply systems that armies have. In other words, the crowd would have had to change its nature and become the thing it fought against.

Still, I understood the desperation and the need to act.

After the Vietnam War, the government made it even easier for the country to continue business as usual: it discontinued the draft. This was, of course, one reason no young man ever walked into my office, demanding I do something to stop the war, as I had done to the pastors of my youth.

Ending the draft was popular with almost everyone: with the young who didn't want to die or to be dragged away from their lives; with the powerful who wanted to get away with murder and thought it would be easier with an all-volunteer force.

Right-wing thinkers of fantasy had never seen that the Vietnam War (like the Iraq War) was a fool's errand, essentially unwinnable on its own terms. They thought by eliminating the students and co-opting the press, as well as ignoring moral standards and the conventions of warfare, American power could only be successful.

The catastrophe of the Iraq War, with its accompanying shadow of torture, should stand forever as the crushing counterexample to that delusion.

But they weren't the only people who believed in the efficacious power of destruction.

I was watching, not long ago, Julie Taymor's wonderful portrait of the sixties (through Beatles' songs!) in her film *Across the Universe*. There's a scene where an angry young woman, whose brother is in Vietnam, shouts at her boyfriend that maybe people would wake up "if the bombs start going off here."

I remembered shouts like that. I remember feeling that logic of a radicalizing movement, and seeing it played out by frustrated people. But radical violence amounted to no real confrontation at all. It's too easy to hate the bombers.

Years later, when a serious, ruthless attack really came here, September 11, 2001, a genuine blowback from our post-Vietnam adventures abroad, all we woke up to was the desire to kill someone in return. As I write (November, 2013), we haven't stopped, and our unmanned drones have made it easier still to go on with our lives and never give our deadly national actions a thought.

IX

During the years I served as a pastor, I knew pastors who fought hard (or maneuvered skillfully) to remove American flags from their sanctuaries, flags the Lutherans I served among had put there, as immigrant communities, precisely to show they were true Americans. I understood why these pastors wanted the flags gone; if I were sitting in their pews, I'd probably support them. But it wasn't a battle I wanted to fight. I thought it would be nearly impossible to get people to understand it, but I may only have been kidding myself. I have to admit I hated conflict and worked to avoid it.

(During the same years, Christian Evangelicals were flying, waving, and even marketing flags any way they could. To them, America was a Christian nation, no more and no less. Like American conservatives in general, they pushed back against the gains made by minorities and women, and against any "liberal" attempts to limit or question American power; they whitewashed American power and disguised it as Christian action in a world that was godless or worse. For most Americans, even for many of the people I served, the Evangelicals simply were, for better or for worse, the public face of the Christian community.)

But flags not only stood in most of our sanctuaries: they were also draped over the coffins of veterans at their funerals. In all the little towns I served, a veteran's coffin bore the flag during the service and was accompanied to the cemetery by a color guard from the local American Legion, complete with rifle salutes and the playing of taps. (Roman Catholics always draped a pall over the coffin during the service, but not even they banned the flag from the graveside ceremony.)

In the second parish I served, the parish the sermons in this book were preached in, we had a lot of funerals during the first year. Our first veteran's funeral was coming up, and I happened to be walking to the post office a few days before it when a large, older man stood in front of me, stopping me, and pointed at my chest.

"What do you think about having the flag on the coffin during a funeral?"

It was a confrontation on the street that I wasn't ready for. I wasn't sure what he was after, so I stuttered a bit. "Um, I—well, we've always had them. I mean, for a veteran—yeah, I assumed there'd be one. Why?"

"So you don't have a problem with them. You're not going to ban them."

"No…um, no, I'm not going to ban them. Why?"

He nodded. "Good. I just wondered."

But I didn't know why he wondered. Later in the week, another man stopped me and asked me the same question.

I asked the funeral director what was going on. He told me the preceding pastor, at his first veteran's funeral, had not allowed the flag to be on the coffin during the service and had provoked an epic battle with the local veterans, a battle the funeral director thought was insane.

I told him I had always gotten along well with veterans groups and that keeping flags off coffins was a battle I had no desire to fight. I agreed that fighting it in a small town, where it had been a beloved custom, was probably hopeless.

Much of the hopelessness comes from the battle being lost already, at the deepest level. Few Christians are able to embrace being a baptized child of God or a disciple of Christ as the deepest thing about themselves, the thing in their lives that consumes them, the thing that remains when

all else is burned away. It's the earthly ties that tug the heart and no one wants to let them go, even, perhaps especially, in the presence of death. One of those ties is military service, and for some people it really is the time they traveled beyond themselves the furthest and sacrificed to something that transcended them. (Reinhold Niebuhr has a profound and provocative sermon titled "The Ark and the Temple," where he argues something like this through the story of King David.)

Another pastor I knew always had the military salute and the presentation of the flag at the graveside done before he did the committal, rather than after. He said he wanted the final word.

Again, I saw his point. But I'm not convinced that this shift in sequence would be powerful and eloquent enough to be worth it. I think most of us die with mixed loyalties because most of us live with them.

I also admit it's hard to say where fooling ourselves begins or ends, and which of our choices is most self-deceiving.

X

In that same parish, whenever I drove back from a visit to the local care center, the first turn I made towards home took me past the Assembly of God church and its parsonage. In election years, the lawn and windows of the parsonage would display the campaign signs of the Republican Party. By the last years of my service, this was unsurprising but still maddening. It always made me grind my teeth.

But once, during the 2004 election, for some reason the Bush-Cheney signs got me thinking about the church in the sixties, about the civil rights movement and the antiwar protests. In those days, it would have been the conservative Christians who were decrying the church's involvement in politics. The Christians who pushed for that involvement often took a warning from the supposed silence of the German church in the thirties, during the rise to power of the Nazi party. It was the failure of the church to speak out, we were told, over and over again, the failure to be involved politically, that allowed that to happen so easily. Christian conservatives could claim they were heeding the same warning the liberals had heeded in the sixties.

The local conservatives could claim they were heeding it more than I was. I regularly, like many Lutherans, gave election-time sermons about Jesus not being a member of any party, about voting as a Christian meaning not voting for a specific party but voting with the needs of your neighbor in mind. No Democratic Party signs appeared on my lawn or my car. We certainly didn't hand out thinly disguised "voting guides." When anyone attended the local party caucuses, which met in the school, they would see members, very active members, of our church in both the Republican and Democratic rooms.

Rightly or wrongly, I thought I could address politics morally and faithfully without supporting specific candidates or programs. Of course, in those polarized years, that in itself became an identifying political position. (More than one person told me I wasn't fooling anybody.) Still, I wanted people of all sorts to feel they were welcome among us. I might say

I wanted, in my sermons, to start people thinking, not stop them from thinking, as our labels and slogans tend to do.

Nevertheless, when I looked at the Assembly of God and its political advertising, I could almost hear them defending their involvement with voices from my youth.

But the day the Bush-Cheney signs sparked my memory, the thought that really came to me was how wrong those voices had been. The religious teachers of my youth had taken the self-serving excuses of the German church—and the German army—at face value. With the sheer horror of the Holocaust and the massive carnage of the war being undeniable, the church and the army purchased a kind of grim, stained nobility for themselves by confessing, on the army's part, too great a sense of duty, and, on the church's part, too timid and deferential a silence. Both implied they knew, and should have done, better.

But as more evidence emerged after the war, it became clear why everyone was so eager to confess they were ignorant, enslaved to duty, afraid, or horribly silent. Those failings would make them look good, compared to what they did.

I had been reading a depressing book called *Betrayal: German Churches and the Holocaust*, edited by Robert Erickson and Susannah Heschel. Instead of a dutiful, silent, but good church, *Betrayal* shows a church all too eager, much of it, to applaud and support what was happening in Germany.

Pastors, on their own, draped the swastika on the altar. The Old Testament was eliminated from classes and church readings. The church celebrated the new Germany and, interestingly enough, justified its actions as "outreach": inviting true Germans to feel at home in a people's church based on blood.

The church didn't betray itself by not speaking. It betrayed itself by what it said.

But this raises a harder question. It's actually easy to understand dutiful, ignorant, fearful, silent people, intimidated or tricked by evil people, by monsters. But what could *attract* all those good *Christians* to Hitler and the Nazi party?

We've demonized the Nazis, and so we don't let ourselves see there was something that *could* attract wide support, something all too familiar. They didn't come proclaiming the pleasures of evil: they came promising goodness, order, renewal, purity; they came promising they'd clean up the place.

All across the world, we see barriers being created between people. From the outside, the ethnic cleansing, the violent oppression, the scorn for right and justice, seem purely evil, horrible. But, from the inside, they're justified by words like order, decency, purity, protection of children, unity of people, the old ways.

Those aren't evil things: that's why they're attractive. What we forget is that they can hide sin and evil as much as anything can: they hide it better because they look so good.

I think one of the bitter lessons of the twentieth century goes beyond being wary of monsters. (We already are.) It's to be wary of those who promise us pure and perfect things, wholesome things, things for the children and the family, especially at the expense of other people. To be wary of ourselves when we want those things desperately, so desperately we don't care how we get them.

When the political advertising of the Assembly of God and the political bullying of Christian conservatives in general infuriated me, it wasn't because of their speaking out. It was because of what they said, what they welcomed as Christian.

XI

I retired in 2010, at the beginning of April. When the end of May came around that year, I was very surprised at how relieved I felt that no one would expect me to show up at the Memorial Day ceremonies and that I would not have to come up with a sermon for the Sunday of that weekend.

At the beginning of my service, Memorial Day at the cemetery was a quiet, peaceful event, and it shared the charm of small-town gatherings like graduations, homecomings, and church anniversaries: you saw another side of the same people you saw everyday; you saw them performing ceremonies themselves, not having them done for them. The pastors of the town would be asked, in turn, to bring prayers and blessings. It was all done seriously and had the rough beauty and the gentle humor of ordinary people trying their best to honor something they cherished.

(I should note, however, to shade my picture a bit, that attendance at

these ceremonies was hardly universal, even among veterans. Small towns and veterans, like family farms and childhood innocence, have been used far too often as political smokescreens by some of our worst political leaders. They're part of the fantasy life of the right-wing demagogues we have in such abundance. So it's worth insisting that neither small towns nor veterans are of one mind about anything. Some of the veterans I knew who had seen the most combat rarely showed up at these ceremonies; my father was one of them. Some of the most vocal and bitter critics of Bush, Cheney, and the Iraq war that I knew were veterans of Korea and Vietnam.)

Still, in my early years as a pastor, Memorial Day at the cemetery was a good time. It was easy to imagine John Ford filming the scene. The sense of the past in a small community that doesn't change much is very strong already: to stand solemnly by the decorated graves, hearing the flags snap in the wind, the bugler playing taps, brought you pretty close to the mystic chords of memory Abraham Lincoln thought were our deepest bonds.

It wasn't so much that this changed or disappeared over the years, but that something grew within it, alongside it, distorting it little by little: a belligerence, an arrogance, a community of sharp division and exclusion.

It might be overstating the case to say we changed, in America, from honoring military service to glorifying war, but that's how it felt sometimes. I remember blurting out once, after listening to one of the speakers, "You know, the highest goal in human life isn't to go halfway around the world to kill somebody."

There has been much written about what happened in America

between the presidencies of Ronald Reagan and George W. Bush: how warfare became constant; how our sense of national identity and national power narrowed to military violence; how democracy at home was warped by imperialism abroad; how no killing, no abuse, no trampling on morality or human rights done by us ever seemed to need accounting.

It was something you could feel at times, even in our small corner of the country, but something you didn't necessarily have to think about. It was all covered with patriotism and the flag, the way the ugliness of the Christian right was covered by the Bible and the cross. You could stay oblivious to the change or even support it, for no other reason than that the words sounded the same.

Thoughts about a changing America were provoked for me by a little reading that started to appear at the Memorial Day ceremonies. I listened to it year after year, saw it printed on editorial pages, and it began to bother me more and more. It's a good example of something that seems respectfully and traditionally patriotic and yet is a glaring display of an embittered, narrowing society.

The reading begins, "It was the veteran, not...," and then line after line is filled in with another vocation and one of the freedoms Americans cherish, thus: it was the veteran, not the poet, who gave us freedom of speech; it was the veteran, not the campus organizer, who gave us the freedom to assemble; it was the veteran, not the lawyer or the politician, who gave us the right to a trial and the right to vote; it was the veteran who gave, while everyone else received.

(I've found two different endings to this: one with a traditional graveside blessing; the other with a bitterly ironic observation that the veteran is buried under the flag so the protester can have the right to burn the flag. The reading seems so much a product of the Vietnam era, both in its polarization and its choice of vocations to exclude—especially "campus organizer"—that it's hard not to think the harsher version was the original. I think, however, the gentler ending was the one I encountered first.)

The first time I heard this, I took it as I thought it was intended, as a tribute. I was a little put off by the negativity, but most graveside tributes deal in overstatement and mourners aren't under oath. (Anyway, I'd be the first to admit that it wasn't the preacher who gave us freedom of religion; most of the history of religion teaches the opposite.)

But what threw me out of the reading and started me chewing on the issues it raised was, oddly enough, the exclusion of the politician and the lawyer. As we walked back to town from the cemetery the first time I heard this, I remarked to somebody that, like it or not, we had to admit that politicians and lawyers really had given us our liberties and rights: people like Jefferson and Madison—nonveterans—had fought to protect them by putting them into law, enshrining them in a Bill of Rights.

But that observation only amounts to a complaint that we shouldn't forget our great thinkers when we're honoring patriots. The more I thought abut the reading, however, and the more times I had to stand silently listening to it, the more false I found it.

Every country in the world has veterans. Our Cold War antagonist, the Soviet Union, was filled with veterans who loved and fought for

Mother Russia in the Second World War. But they enjoyed few of our rights and liberties. If it was the veteran who gave those things, they should have had them.

Over the years of the Iraq catastrophe, our country was creating more veterans; yet, under the same administration that led us to war, American liberties were shrinking. American troops were fighting constantly, but it was getting harder to say they were fighting for anybody's freedom, including our own.

What finally bothered me the most about that reading was how narrow a vision it had of our country, how dismissive it was toward the contributions, the patriotic actions, of so many people.

Think again of Jefferson and Madison. Now consider further: by themselves, they couldn't force civil liberties and civil rights into law. People had to vote for that Bill of Rights, people who cared about freedom as much as they did. All sorts of people fought for rights in all sorts of ways: teachers, reformers, medical workers, police officers, firefighters, community builders, artists, farmers, construction workers, ordinary people of decent character. (No doubt a few preachers as well. Martin Luther King Jr., say.) Furthermore, those rights have to be continually defined and defended in the courts by lawyers and judges, and in the legislatures by politicians—and, once again, by voters. For much of the twentieth century, it was the American Civil Liberties Union, not the VFW or the American Legion, that worked to extend those rights.

It's simply false to say that no one but the veteran contributed to American freedom. What bothered me about the reading—the narrow vision of community, the exclusion, the belligerence, the militarism—was what was bothering me about the country.

XII

I have tried to give some sense, in the preceding pages, of the person I was and perhaps some sense as well of the community I served during those years of war. As I said, this writing took shape because I thought that what a pastor like me found to say on Memorial Day weekend in one small-town church pulpit might say something about the time. I have gathered the sermons for five of those Sundays in Part III, "Memory."

As these were intended as part of the historical record, I have resisted the almost overwhelming temptation to rewrite or edit them. Except for anything I might have added or changed delivering them, they are pretty much the words I spoke on those days. I should note, too, that in the tradition I served in, the readings for each Sunday are set by a three-year lectionary. Thus, I didn't choose the texts I spoke on. I always thought it made for an interesting dialogue to accept whatever text arose and set it against the happenings of the day. Also, on any given Sunday in a parish, there is usually more than one thing going on that must be addressed. I have added a brief note before each sermon to illuminate the context.

Those sermons weren't easy to write. At the time, the war troubled me, the gospel accused me, more and more. But I was very aware that many of those sitting in the pews before me felt neither troubled nor accused and saw nothing wrong with America's wars, if they thought about them at all. I believe I've already said I hated conflict and tried hard to avoid it.

I might say, given the other voices we all were hearing, that I tried to speak more broadly about faith and life and more realistically about war. But the real effect of Christian preaching is not for the preacher to judge.

In Part II, "War," I have added, for further background, a newsletter column I wrote in the run-up to the Iraq war and the sermon I gave the Sunday after it began.

In Part IV, "Judgment," I have added some concluding remarks on how things seem to me, looking back.

Conservative Christians have conferred a presumptive moral palatability on any occasion on which the United States resorts to force. They have fostered among the legions of believing Americans a predisposition to see U.S. military power as inherently good, perhaps even a necessary adjunct to the accomplishment of Christ's saving mission.

—Andrew Bacevich, *The New American Militarism*

Church Newsletter, October, 2002

I got sick of hearing the Bush administration's push for war with Iraq compared to Churchill's stand against Hitler's Germany. We had a monthly newsletter with a Pastor's column, so in October, 2002, I thought I'd give at least my circle of readers a more detailed picture of the real Churchill's reflections on Munich, from his history of the war. I might also have noted that in the preface to the same work, Churchill said the Second World War should have been called "The Unnecessary War", since there "never was a war more easy to stop." One suspects, in Iraq's case, that the diplomatic pressure and the weapons inspections being carried on by the UN—and thwarted by the United States—would have been closer to what Churchill had in mind. If people needed a comparison from that era, the German propaganda assault before the invasion of Poland would seem to be more apt, though admittedly not of much use to the Bush government.

I've been listening to all the war discussions with sorrow and apprehension. (I was tempted to say "everyone has been," but I hate to sound stupid in print.) In fact, fretting over Israel, I've been hoping and praying for some path to peace to appear in that region for some time.

I don't think Christians need to be apologetic for lifting their voices for peace in any conflict, great or small. On the other hand, we don't like to sound—or to be!—stupid either, and the claims of realism, practicality and worldly wisdom often seem to lie wholly with the voices of force.

We're still haunted by the ghosts of the twentieth century, especially the failure of the nations to stand up to Hitler's Germany. Every few days, in the news, someone will refer to the yielding of Britain at Munich or to Churchill's opposing call to arms.

But I happened to be reading Churchill's war memoirs this summer, and—after he discussed Munich—he paused, unusually, to "set down some principles of morals and action" as a future guide.

First, he insists, with decisions like this, the circumstances make all the difference. Second, obviously, the future is unknown: thus, our choices depend greatly on our general feelings and aims. Then he says this:

> Those who are prone by temperament and character to seek sharp and clear-cut solutions of difficult and obscure problems, who are ready to fight whenever some challenge comes from a foreign power, have not always been right. On the other hand, those whose inclination is to bow their heads, to seek patiently and faithfully for peaceful compromise, are not always wrong. On the contrary, in the majority of instances they may be right, not only morally but from a practical standpoint. How many wars have been averted by patience and persisting good will! Religion and virtue alike lend their sanctions to meekness and humility, not only between men but between nations. How many wars have been precipitated by firebrands! How many misunderstandings which led to wars could have been removed by temporizing!

It's not surprising that he goes on to say that, nevertheless, national leaders aren't Quakers and must be prepared for force as a last resort, and that this case was a time for it. What is surprising was that he paused, after being the prophet who'd been proved right, to lift up this tribute to peacemakers as a caution.

In other words, for Churchill himself, the lesson of Munich was not to be ready to fight every challenge. The peacemakers did not err in principle, but in judgment of the circumstances. Most surprising to me was this statement: "On the contrary, in the majority of instances, they may be right, not only morally but from a practical standpoint."

An interesting reflection, from someone we usually think of as a bellicose, swashbuckling imperialist. And something to keep in mind when pondering realism and ideals.

No one knows where our present perils will lead us. Christians have found themselves swept up in wars, found themselves driven to wars, and will again. But we hear the call of a greater voice, too, and hopes and prayers for peace are always important: as a witness and as a realistic caution, as a moderating influence within conflict, as a goal for its end, and as healing for its aftermath.

See you in church.

Iraq War, March, 2003

This sermon was given March 23, 2003, the Sunday after the Iraq war began. It was the third Sunday in Lent. The question that begins the sermon is from the second lesson for that day, Paul's First Epistle to the Corinthians, 1:18–25. The gospel reading is John 2:13–22, Jesus cleansing the temple, and the remarks about the ten commandments refer to the first reading, Exodus 20:1–17. I should note that, though my son was in the Marine Corps during the First Gulf War, his unit was never sent to Iraq. At the time, however, I didn't know this, and my anxiety remained a vivid memory for me.

"Where is the one who is wise?"

That question Paul cries out in the second lesson might be one leaping from a lot of tongues in our uncertain world. And when he continues "Has not God made foolish the wisdom of the world?" you wonder why God bothered, because we usually do a pretty good job of that ourselves.

But Paul really doesn't expect anyone to come forward and show their smarts. And the last thing he's interested in is encouraging one human genius against another.

It's a question of dismissal, a question of contempt, a ridiculing of human cleverness and power and pride *as such* before the mystery of the cross. It's a declaration of *all* humanity's limits, the horizon of ignorance and powerlessness that's always closer than we think.

Sitting under the cross, making that confession, is probably not a bad place to be in the first week of war.

We knew it was coming. Some of us dreaded it, some cheered it, some thought it a step into disaster, some thought it grimly necessary. But now it just is, and it's ours. Somebody said we don't agree on the war, but we all agree on the peace: we want it to be soon, with few American casualties, few civilian casualties, and a stable settlement for the future. That "we *all* agree" might be a little strong to claim as you get further on in that list. But it's a reasonable hope and it's a good hope, and I share it.

Most of us have mixed feelings. Our son was in the Marines during the First Gulf War and I'll never forget being glued to CNN at 2:00 in the morning trying to spot somebody from the 3rd Recon Battalion. You're proud of them for their service, you want them to be there, but you're anguished about their danger, and you *don't* want them to be there. Our leaders may think the world's black and white, but the world of a soldier's parents is pretty gut-level grey.

I dreaded this one: I think we've been flooded with partial truths and wishful thinking—our popular media told us more in the last ten years abut Bill Clinton's underwear than it has about the Arab world. But once the troops go, my heart goes with them. When I hear "101st Airborne" or

"a 7th Cavalry column"—these units that echo in American history—I get this primal rush of identification. Go get 'em! I want them to win, because they're ours.

You hope the government feels that way, too. How exactly do you send these kids into the desert and the same week submit a budget that cuts veterans' benefits? (Man, how do politicians sleep?)

We can't do much but watch and pray, but it's the *ending* that will need our prayers and our watching.

I was at the dentist a few weeks ago—when it was still: will we? won't we? (or people thought it was)—and the assistant was doing whatever they do in your mouth. (Why do they always ask you questions when you've got a mouthful of instruments?) But she said: "Oh, I'm so tired of hearing about Iraq, and talking about Iraq: why don't we just do it and get it over with?" I almost swallowed the drill.

Over with? In 1967, Israel fought a short, six-day war—less than a week! Time to shower for the Sabbath!—little Israel: demolished the Arabs—Egypt! Jordan! Syria!—took East Jerusalem, the West Bank, Gaza strip and the Sinai peninsula, got it done. They fought a harder one in '73, but really, militarily, in those territories it was done, thirty years ago. Is it over in Israel? Their life's been a nightmare and there's no army for them to finish off: just one suicidally hateful teenager after another. They won the war but they lost the peace, and we hope we don't.

But even in the best cases, at the personal level, there's a cost: the last few years, you've been able to watch interviews on the History Channel with the wonderful, old World War II vets: they talk about things that happened fifty years ago as though they happened yesterday (my father was the same way—that was life!): and after they've lived fifty *years* of calm, peaceful lives, some of them still can't talk without weeping. And those are the survivors *who are whole*. For them, it's never over. That's the cost of these things. That's why we honor these guys.

That was the voice of complacency—"get it over with"—and the voice of privilege, where most of us are lucky that we never have to see the consequences. That's the lesson we *should* have learned on September 11, 2001.

It's *understandable* that people are frustrated by tension and are relieved by action. That's an almost physical part of any decision you've been bothered by. But was I the only one who felt scuzzy when the stock market went *up* as we sent our people into danger? Or flabbergasted when stock analysts said, "Well, the uncertainty's over"?

Really.

It's the *ending* of the combat that's an abyss of uncertainty. And the world is more uncertain. Internationally, it's in shreds.

I'll speak from a parent's perspective. Probably everybody knows our daughter worked in the World Trade Center complex, and she's still in New York. (In the financial district. She takes the subway every day that goes under the river—imagine how vulnerable that is!) They know they're a target. Back when that attack happened, I was grateful for the worldwide outpouring of outrage and sympathy. We all were! Even the miserable French—"Nous sommes tous les Americains"—"We're all Americans." And I was *absolutely certain* that, if there was another strike, there would be the same outpouring *and* the real cooperation. "What do you need? What can we do?"

If there were a strike tomorrow on New York, could any of us be *certain* we'd get the same scale of sympathy and support? I'm not. Right or wrong's beside the point. That's a loss, it's a real loss, it's a grievous loss. You can say it had to be, but to say it doesn't matter is breathtakingly shortsighted.

So we watch and pray and hope for good. Our lives have to go on—and ours have to go on as people of faith.

It *may* seem foolish, as the apostle Paul well knew, to turn to the cross in times of anxiety and uncertainty, to gather under this symbol of weakness and loss. And yet, how strange, it's often just those times we turn to the cross most fervently, and find our hope steadied, find the strength to carry on through the wrecks of time. Christians have lived through times of uncertainty before, for centuries. In a way, before the cross, Christian faith is *about* the bottom dropping out of life and time, all times, anxious times and complacent times; it's as much a judgment as a promise; it declares the limits of our strength and wisdom; it's about the bottom dropping out of life and living on in hope anyway. We get strength in anxious times by returning and clinging to what we do in ordinary times.

As I was walking around early last week, *feeling* like the bottom was dropping out of life, I found myself looking forward to today's service—"this is my anchor!": and when I glanced at the gospel, I thought: great! Jesus goes to church! What a fine role model! For young and old!

But then I read on: Jesus goes to church?! Jesus goes berserk! I was hoping for something a little more comforting, like the Good Shepherd! Or: "Let not your hearts be troubled!" Or—well, a lot of others I can think of!

It's the kind of scene that would send you running back to the ten commandments, if you were looking for security.

It's pretty violent for Jesus. It seems like a moment of madness, just about the only one I can think of, an explosion of all too human frustration, righteous anger run amuck. Imagine this happening at the WELCA bazaar!

It's had a weird history of interpretation. It's been taken as an endorsement of violence or righteous force. In fact, just a couple weeks ago, a letter in the Minneapolis Star mentioned it: "See—Jesus went to war." (It's not the first time it's been taken that way.) It's been used by the radical Christians of the Reformation, who smashed statues and stained-glass windows in churches. On the other side of the political spectrum, there was a British pacifist sculptor after World War I named Eric Gill who got a commission for a war memorial at Leeds University: when it was unveiled, it showed this scene: but Jesus whipping *people* out of the temple, and the people were dressed as British aristocrats and British bankers with top hats and carrying ledger books with the British monetary symbols on them. Since the people who paid for the memorial were aristocrats and bankers whose sons had died in the war, you can imagine that went over like a lead duck.

But just how mad was Jesus? And, mad or not, what exactly was this about? This scene is in every gospel, but those aren't easy questions to answer.

In the other gospels, it happens almost at the end, so it's easy to take it as an uncontrollable outburst after building frustration. But here it's very early, John *chapter two*; and when the people ask him, "Well, what's your sign for doing this?" it implies *they* don't see it as an uncontrollable outburst but as a calculated act.

To state the obvious: this isn't about war or the social effects of commerce: it's something about the temple, the heart of faith. And, to put it in the terms I've been stewing about, I think it's about the certainties of life and faith, and where they're found, and where they're not.

Jesus had a complicated attitude toward the temple, and it's something the New Testament writers can shade different ways: there are strongly anti-temple statements in the New Testament, and there are strong claims of continuity.

But Jesus shared the old prophetic quarrel with the temple that shows up in Jeremiah, Isaiah, Amos, Malachi, the quarrel of more spiritual faith with a kind of external faith that's too satisfied with observances and is not of the heart. Christians have continued that quarrel in his very footsteps.

But there are a couple of things to notice about what he's driving out. He's not mad about the money because it's money: they *changed* money because Gentiles *and their coins* weren't allowed inside—so it was a sign or, well, a *literal barrier* of exclusivity: it kept the temple from being a "house of prayer for all nations" (in that old prophetic dream). And he drives out *sheep and cattle* because they were actually sacrificed in the temple and—though no one could possibly see this—*his sacrifice* would replace them as the way to God.

So he's pointing the worship of the temple towards a worship that's open to all, that's of spirit and truth, and that is founded on a life, a *way*, of sacrifice. But he's claiming a *continuity*, a *fulfillment*.

I think if you asked anybody there that day: Which makes you feel more secure—this building of stone, the literal *house* of the Lord, the ceremonies of sacrifice where you can see the real flesh and blood of these animals offered, *or this guy*, and whatever it is he wants? No contest. *Anybody* would take the stone and the cattle.

And yet the temple is gone, as any of our houses of worship can go, and the spirit of Christ lives on.

But even Christians: if, like me on Tuesday, they were asked to look at these *lessons* and say where they found the most certainty, the most security, I imagine most would say the ten commandments. I did that! "Oh, what a relief! The ten commandments! Security blanket! Home! Familiarity!" That's what people want to put on school walls, not pictures of Jesus overturning tables and swinging a whip like Indiana Jones.

But we rarely see them written all the way out, so we can forget how much of them are simply about turning to God, and very much an inner turning, of the spirit, of memory—eleven verses out of seventeen. And we forget the Israelites got these on a journey, a wandering in the wilderness, when in fact they did not feel very secure most of the time.

And that wilderness journey was part of that longer Biblical journey. And we say: that journey ends in the cross.

It's always hard to realize that when Paul says "God's foolishness is wiser than human wisdom and God's weakness is stronger than human strength," he's talking about the sacrifice of the cross: that he doesn't mean God will help us figure things out when we give up, or that God will slug the enemies we can't handle, and so we'll still win *on our terms*, but that the way of Christ really does look foolish and weak, to *everybody*. And yet: *there* is strength, *there* is the bedrock of hope, *there* is life.

At the heart of Jesus' outburst in the temple is that summons to find our true certainty there: that, before God, there is no substitute for that yielding of the heart, that leap of faith, the something within that allows God's wisdom and courage to flow into us.

We come to places like this, we come to church, to faith, part building, part journey, for lots of reasons. What happens as we live in faith, I think, is that we're *given* reasons why we're here. I was tempted when I started writing to say: one of those reasons we come, that we're given, over time, is to learn to *live with* uncertainty. But that's not quite accurate. We're called to see *human* life, *all* human life, as uncertain, that nobody's wisdom or strength is smart enough or strong enough to be invulnerable to fortune. But we're called to live in the certainty of Christ crucified, the power of God which looks so foolish to a world that's always perishing, and yet, in its mystery, is the way to life.

Amen.

III. MEMORY

You drop a bomb and it falls on the just and the unjust.

—Isidor Rabi, on his reluctance to work on the
 Manhattan Project

2003

This sermon was given May 25, 2003. It was the sixth Sunday of Easter and the gospel text was John 15: 9-17.

Back before we went to seminary, I worked for a few years as a pipefitter and a thermostat mechanic—of all things—with Purdue University's physical plant. Most of the older workers were men my father's age, and most of them had seen some sort of service in the Second World War. We had quite a cross-section of service branches and theatres of operation, and that experience was still very vivid for them. Listening to the talk during coffee breaks was like sitting in on a super History seminar on military life in that war.

The man I helped was an almost incomprehensible southerner from Taswell, Tennessee. I can still see myself the first day staring at a tool box trying to figure out what on earth he wanted when he yelled for a "pop" wrench, until one of the other guys said, "He's trying to say 'pipe,' kid. We can't understand him either." He's the only person I've ever heard in real life seriously call someone else a "blackguard." Everybody called him "Stumpy" and I was "Doc" and, since we were the smallest people in a shop full of gorillas, we'd often be ridiculed as two of the seven dwarves.

He had been a tank driver in the Marine Corps on Iwo Jima, then served in China before that collapsed. He had intended to be a career marine until they made him a guard in a military prison. For such a roughneck, he had a gentle heart, so he could never look on the prisoners as guilty but only as "good ole boys who'd had a little hard luck." He kept smuggling in treats for them, wouldn't enforce the regulations, and finally quit.

One day, we were sitting with a couple of the painters, and he got to talking with one of them who'd also driven a tank in the war. The painter had a thick accent, too, which I couldn't place at first: he sounded like one of my older relatives. But as they compared experiences, terrors, hairy moments, I realized this guy had fought on the Russian front in the *German* army. He'd come over here in the fifties—for a better life.

They had that soldiers' bond, of experience, terror, and, I guess, survival, a country of their own, a living memory that civilians of both countries can't really share the same way. I suppose you could say they had to do a little forgetting of antagonisms to share those memories quite so easily. They found a common bond beneath the antagonisms. You might think on days like Memorial Day the German painter would be a little to one side of things emotionally. Maybe. But human nature is richer and stranger, more oddly and widely attached than we want to think. It *gets* attached.

The painter's children—certainly his grandchildren—will sound, think, and they will *feel* pretty much like the rest of us. They'll just *be* Americans. This is a big country, with a lot of ways into it, and we sometimes forget that.

I was amused, a couple of weeks ago, to read about a little encounter Donald Rumsfeld, the Defense Secretary, had with our common past. He was at a press conference where he was praising our all-volunteer army, certainly praiseworthy, and the subject of conscription, the draft, came up, and he said, no, we really didn't need that—and that's fair enough, as a position; but then he said... (And I have to admit I have some public speaker's sympathy with him, because I've done the same dumb thing: you've made your point and then some evil demon whispers in your ear 'Hey! Use *this* example! It'll really nail your argument!' and the minute you say it, or an hour later, or the next day, you realize 'Oh, no! That proved exactly the opposite of what I wanted to say! I hope no one noticed!'—and, of course, someone always does.) So: he dismissed the draft; but then he said, "Look at Vietnam: draftees really added no value, no advantage to the armed services for any length of time." That bothered somebody enough that they did a little research and pointed out that of the 58,000 names of the dead on the Vietnam wall, 20,000 or so were draftees. They at least contributed the value of 20,000 lives.

Donald Rumsfeld doesn't strike me as somebody who apologizes easily, but he did apologize to veterans' organizations in this case. It was the voice of the dead that forced it, speaking through the memory of the living. It wasn't about policy anymore, it was about memory.

It's easy to forget, under the pressure of the present moment, under the pressure of what we want right now, all that's gone into who we are. A couple of years ago, there was a movie out called *Glory* about some all-black regiments that fought in the Civil War, and a lot of people were surprised to learn that blacks *had* fought as regular troops at all. They suffered horrendous casualties and weren't treated as prisoners of war. So it was quite a sacrifice for them. This is a big country, and a lot of different people have loved it for a lot of different reasons.

The blacks in *Glory* couldn't have loved it for what happened to them: they loved it for its promise, and hope. My grandparents loved it for its economic opportunities. Some loved the beauty of the landscape, the openness, free ranges. Some loved the freedom from persecution of one sort or another. All those loves can be *called* freedom, but they can also fight with each other pretty bitterly. If you watch closely, every Western movie ever made shows two of those loves, and sometimes three, in conflict: the mountain men, the settlers and small farmers, the cattle barons—all crying freedom. I suppose democracy could be defined as an unending argument about what that means. But we do find a common bond in memory, a bond with the dead, those who struggled in lots of ways to get us here, and it can bind us beneath our antagonisms.

Memory is such a mystery, what the heart gets attached to. My own family wasn't here before the start of the last century, so our real connection to America started with speakeasies and bootleggers in Chicago. But if I read about life in Poland in 1850, it leaves me cold. Whereas if I watch a movie like *Young Mr. Lincoln*, with Henry Fonda as Honest Abe, and he's walking up the hill at the end, and a storm is coming, and you hear *The Battle Hymn of the Republic, that's* when I can get choked up. *That* seems like *mine*—through a common memory *acquired* here (even though *we* weren't here *then*).

It's good to keep that memory big and roomy. Memorial Day started after the civil war, but it's grown to embrace all wars, and really, I think, all the dead—so that people dress up their own people's graves, military and otherwise, as an honor to the past.

It's probably impossible for any of us to look at today's gospel reading, on Memorial Day weekend, without having one verse jump out at us: "No one has greater love than this, to lay down one's life for one's friends." And the passage does echo with themes of sacrifice, love, memory, continuity, the passing on of a gift, the abiding in a heritage.

It certainly treasures all those human things and impulses. But, like all the calls of Jesus, it broadens them and lifts them to a higher plane, by putting them in the light of the purposes and the love of God.

Christians, in their funny way, have formed an odd sort of community in time, floating across centuries and continents, with all the human attachments we have but also with a tug on our hearts from the kingdom not of this world. Though we speak of the "Holy Land," there's really no landscape attached to our identity—no sights or smells, not even a peculiar language, unless we count the inside of our own churches, the rhythms of our own Bible translations, but then we know they all count equally, from Minnesota to Egypt. We don't really have tribal boundaries, though we always get mixed up with them. But we know, if we're pushed—and I suppose we always have to be pushed—that we carry that divine call to find a common bond with all others, all the children of God, to find our way to love. The way Peter did in the first lesson: Can we deny *these guys* since the Spirit came to them, too?

In a way, the call of Christ asks us to find the peace and acceptance with the living that we find with the past and the dead.

There's a famous speech in Shakespeare's play *The Merchant of Venice* about common bonds in life. The play's about some Christians who get in trouble with a Jewish moneylender, Shylock, and there's a lot of tribal antagonism in it. At one point, Shylock, defending himself, says this:

> "Hath not a Jew eyes? hath not a Jew hands, organs, dimensions, senses, affections, passions? fed with the same food, hurt with the same weapons, subject to the same diseases, healed by the same means, warmed and cooled by the same winter and summer, as a Christian is? If you prick us, do we not bleed? If you tickle us, do we not laugh? If you poison us, do we not die?"

Shylock's really appealing to the commonality of *biological* life, something we share as unquestionably as we will share death. The problem is that most of what we *call* life—with its passions and struggles, attachments and antagonisms—is lived in that great arena *between* biology and death, forgetful of both shared extremes.

Jesus calls us to enter that arena of human interaction, human life together, with the quality of *love*—to find a commonality through that force that will sometimes require sacrifice of us. But this is God's life, this is what the life of God is—above the flesh and *beyond* death: and what our life together, as we abide in God's life, can be. This quality of life, this ideal, this way of acting and believing—this too can be common.

Maybe we should call that the Christian dream. It's a point where a lot of thoughtful people have declared the Christian faith to be simply impossible, because it's in the nature of love to be exclusive. "*This* is mine, not *that*." In fact, this passage is often used at weddings, when we certainly *do* expect the particular love in question at that moment to *be* exclusive.

And, to be honest, it's one of the ironies of John's gospel and John's epistles that they are the most intimate and warm expressions of the communion of love in the New Testament and, at the same time, they have been the most divisive, the most polarizing, the most sweeping in denouncing enemies, the most quick to call others "the children of the devil."

Luther would say: we see again that the call of the gospel reveals our sin. But I don't think it has to mean we can't ever overcome it, and Christians *have* managed at times to cross the boundaries of antagonism.

But we can't confuse our desires with God's. For all the intimacy offered here, for all the welcome into the circle of God's life, the blurring really of the divine-human boundary, the encouragement of power and authority in the believer, still, still, for all that, authority still goes only one way—from God to us. He says, "You didn't choose me—I chose you." He calls them "friends" but he's careful to say, "You are my friends *if you do what I command you.*"

Well! If one of your merely human friends ever said that to you, I'd think you'd be reevaluating that friendship pretty fast. But that's the point here: this is a unique relationship. And there's a difference between entering God's life and reducing God's life to ours. For all the intimacy granted, one partner is supreme.

We would probably, at times, all *like* to say something like that: "you're my friend *if* you do what I command you." (If we said it to our spouses, we'd get a frying pan in the back of the head.) But every pastor, every leader, would love to be able to get away with saying, "We'll get along just fine if I always get my way." (That's probably the verse in the passage that jumps out at *government officials*. Come to think of it, John 15:14 would make a pretty accurate motto for American foreign policy!)

When I was thinking about this passage, I was reminded of possibly my most favorite moment in a presidential election. It was when Ross Perot was running—in... what? '92? His running mate was Admiral Stockdale, a good man, war hero—and I was watching a debate between the vice-presidential candidates. Stockdale criticized the gridlock in Washington and he said: "When I commanded a ship, I could get things done because my word was law—one man in charge: gave an order and it was done. Right down the chain of command."

I was kind of nodding along, thinking this blunt old warrior was making sense. Then it struck me that what Stockdale was really saying was that our entire Constitution, with its balance of powers, and 200 years of democratic experience were colossal mistakes and that we'd all be better off with an Absolute Monarchy or a (presumably benevolent) dictatorship. That was an extraordinarily candid admission by a major candidate. (They all want to act like emperors—but not many will say so.)

It's worth remembering that a lot of absolute monarchs in history have had their heads chopped off. Also, that the world is full of military dictatorships and those are just the countries people run away from. And, anyway, of all the reasons there are to love our big, messy, brawling country, one of them is probably *not* that one person can tell all the rest of us what to think and what to do. America's sort of been about something else.

I think one of the great gifts this Christian call to love can give us, can give any community, can give our earthly loves, is an indirect gift. The supremacy of God's love, that insistence that only God can ask that absolute obedience, is a blessing to our little loves because it limits them. And it ought to limit the damage we do to each other when our limited loves clash.

The claim of Jesus on us, the call to us to approach one another in love, is really a call to see all our attachments as limited. I like to think that's not so foreign to what a democracy asks of us, at its best: to put up with one another, if nothing else, for the common good. I like to think we've flourished here because our old eternal call to love has found a kind of echo in a society a lot of people have struggled, and died, to make an open and tolerant place.

We can always fail because we always remain sinful. When we get scared or divided, it's easy to forget our ideals. But all our arguments, at bottom, are about who we are, who we're going to be, and about who we've been. It's important that we remember largely and generously.

Here we offer our reminder to love one another as Christ loved us, that among all our strivings this is the fruit *we* were appointed to bear, through that claim of Christ, and that this is one of the best gifts we Christians can give to any land we sojourn in.

Amen.

2004

This sermon was given May 30, 2004. That Sunday also happened to be the Feast of Pentecost, with the key reading for the day being the story of Pentecost in Acts 2:1–21. The quotation from Jesus I begin with is from the gospel of the day, John 14:8–7, 25–27. We had recently had a large funeral for a well-beloved member, something which tends to be on people's minds at the Sunday service. Something else on most people's minds was the recent revelation of the abuse of prisoners by US troops at the Abu Ghraib prison.

I notice that I referred to the "War Department" in my story about John Huston's film Let There Be Light. *The title "War Department" at least had a blunt honesty; the change to "Department of Defense," after the National Security Act of 1947, marks a stage in the history of American hypocrisy.*

[Jesus said] "The Holy Spirit…will remind you of all that I have said to you. Peace I leave with you; my peace I give to you.…Do not let your hearts be troubled, and do not let them be afraid."

When those words rise up from a biblical reading, I don't need a special act of the Holy Spirit to stir the pool of memory. They are familiar words among Christians. We turn to them often at times of death, speak them on the day of burial, and living in those days of loss releases a flood of memory, past joys and sorrows, all dimmed with the sadness of the past, things that can't be changed and won't come back.

We just read that passage at Amos Blombeck's funeral, and we find ourselves now on Memorial Day weekend, when we willingly enter the company of the lost as a community, decorate their graves and claim our bond with those who are gone.

And when we were discussing Amos's funeral with Gary and Brenda, my own memory was stirred by his obituary highlighting that he had served in the Navy on the flagship at Iwo Jima. I've known fairly well two of the marines who were in that battle—one I worked with at Purdue a couple of years, one a retired farmer up North (who always wore that flag-raising pin on Sunday)—and for both of them that battle, more than the service itself, was the most defining, most vivid time in their lives.

When I was a kid, everybody knew—and I hope they still do—the photograph of the five marines raising the flag on Mount Suribachi that became the model for the Marine Corps monument in Arlington. It may not be the grandest or the most moving monument, but I've always thought it was the most inspiring, with that inscription: Uncommon Valor was a Common Virtue. It can still give me chills. (It's a picture you're happier remembering than some others we've seen.)

A lot of speeches cluster around Memorial Day, talk about ideals and philosophies, things that might be said on the Fourth of July: but this is a quieter day, with something wordless about it. The emotional center, I think, lies beneath declarations and ideals and has more to do with simple belonging and loss—just: these were ours, they were lost.

Soldiers go off for lots of reasons: some idealists; some from simple duty, not really wanting to; some not to miss it; some because they wanted a better life—minorities trying to make it in a society that mostly doesn't want them; college students trying to pay their way. They're not as simple and homogeneous as we civilians sometimes make them sound.

And, in a democracy, soldiers don't design the policies or the brilliant plans. They just pay for them. We shouldn't confuse the two, one way or the other. I've heard some soldiers say they feel they have more in common with the soldiers on the other side than they do with the civilians of either, and there's something about this Memorial observance that draws us toward a place *like that*.

Because of that elemental gathering back, gathering in, the Day has been able to expand from its Civil War roots—still echoed in those letters G.A.R. (the Grand Army of the Republic)—and embrace not just the two sides of *that* horrible division, but the dead of other wars, and really all the lost—people go out to tend all their graves, military or not. It's become a kind of National Day of the Dead, a day of memory and peace, a day of grace beyond strife.

Those words—peace, grace—draw us close to what we're about here. In the Christian community, we live by memory—we learn things, in that wonderful phrase, "by heart"—we *make* the words of the past familiar, not just in reverence for the past, but in the hope that they light the future and carry us into eternity.

And through nothing but the mysteries of the shifting Christian calendar, we also find ourselves celebrating the Day of Pentecost (—that's why I'm decked out in this alluring red): an event from our past called up not just for honoring but for guiding: to show the nature of *this* community, what the church is or ought to be.

Now Pentecost was not a day of common fate, but of the new and strange: the wind and fire of the spirit, the miracle of languages. But it was a day alive to human division—all these nations gathered—and brought its own charge, its own power and pointing of the way to the healing of divisions.

Many in the church remember Pentecost for its excitement—there are churches called "Pentecostal" which my mother used to call "Holy Rollers," and every time we drove past a little cinder block church near our house I'd hope to see people somersaulting out the windows. But Luke spends more time on the meaning than the excitement: and the deeper things to remember are the understanding that takes place, that coming of the Spirit that enables the cowardly Peter to speak, the gathering into Christ beyond the tongues and the tribes of the earth.

But what struck me this week was Peter's use of memory: this is a long speech in Acts and we only have part of it—but even here you can see he's calling up things from their past: "Remember the prophet Joel? Well, these *are* those last days. Don't wait for anything else." And I wish we had the next part in our reading, but right after this he talks about Jesus: "Remember the guy that did all those wonders, those healings?—well, he was from God and 'this man...*you* crucified, *you* killed.'"

He's opening the past for them: but this wouldn't have been long after the crucifixion: he's using memory as a *judgment* and an *accusation*. To move them toward God: he goes on to tie this event of the Spirit to Jesus and ends up baptizing them when they ask "What should we do?"

But how is it that this can be the final thing of life? How can those days—in 30 something AD—be or begin the *last days* of all of us? And why would anyone *need* to hear this? Why would *we*? Why should *this* be the center of all our living?

Well: could there be something wrong at the heart of the world that we're never going to solve?

Maybe we don't remember enough.

Our feelings this Memorial Day have to be a little more raw and edgy, because the nation won't be gathering only around weathered gravestones that were laid down before the children in the High School band were born. There are new ones every week somewhere, and there will be more.

You can tell by the swings in public opinion that we don't remember how horrible and how costly war is. After both the world wars of the last century, there were people who seriously thought war had become impossible: that no one sane would ever risk it again, because the suffering and the horrors were on such a scale they could never be forgotten.

But of course they were.

We forget how unpredictable war is. We laugh bitterly at the stories of the leaders and generals who said in 1861 or 1914 or 1944 or 1967 that victory was around the corner, there was light at the end of the tunnel, and the troops would be home by Christmas—and then we listen to them all over again.

We forget the horrible damage weapons, bombs can do. One of the things that's really bothered me in the newspapers has been the seeming dismissal of actions in which "there were none killed but only a few wounded": wounded—that hides a world of pain. War wounds are horrible. Mothers are coming back who won't walk, fathers who won't see. Worse. The same things happen to the civilians who are unlucky enough to get in the way.

We recoil from that: we don't want to think about it.

At the end of World War II, the movie director John Huston—he made *The Maltese Falcon*, *The African Queen*, *The Treasure of the Sierra Madre*: a great director!—was in the Army Signal Corps, making documentaries. And he got involved in making one at an Army hospital, showing how they were rehabilitating soldiers who'd suffered mental damage—people who couldn't stop shaking, couldn't talk without stuttering, who were paralyzed—not physically but so traumatized they couldn't get their limbs to move. The doctors had 6–8 weeks, to do what they could.

Huston and his crew followed one group from arrival to departure, ran the cameras all the time, then cut it down to an hour: they called it *Let There Be Light*. It was a tribute to what these men had been through and what these doctors had been able to restore. The beginning is painful, but the joy you see at the end is overwhelming—it *was* a tribute.

So they showed it to the War Department. The story goes that some generals walked out because they had no idea what men had gone through. They buried the film, wouldn't release it—they told Huston it was a "privacy" issue, even though all the men had signed releases—because they didn't want anyone else to know how bad it was.

I saw it about thirty years or so after it was made—I believe Hubert Humphrey was one of the people who worked to get it finally released. But, in the meantime, we fought a couple more wars where stress and trauma were more easily spoken of—and you *would* occasionally hear someone say "Well, you never heard about this in World War II and that generation." It wasn't because it didn't happen—we decided to forget it. It didn't fit the heroic picture. (And that's a betrayal of those who suffered—and those who will.)

I don't know that Americans are any worse than anyone else on that score, though some people accuse us of being so. A very clever American writer named Gore Vidal says the 'A' in USA should stand for Amnesia because we're always being surprised and shocked by things that happened before or things we should have seen coming.

I'll tell one on myself. Shortly after the September 11 attacks, I was listening to some radio panel discussion about terrorism coming here and how it was a new experience for us, to feel this indiscriminate hatred coming at us, out of the blue. And there was an old black pastor on the panel, who must have been squirming in his seat, and he finally said: "It's a new experience for *you*. *We* know—the black community knows—terrorism's always been here." And he started to talk about lynchings, mutilations, torture, black churches being fire-bombed, the church where some little girls were killed in Sunday School. And, you know, I felt ashamed because I'd known that and I'd forgotten it, and I certainly never put it together with the sense we had of being the target of some other people's hatred—that there were people living here who felt like that for a long time and could feel that way looking at someone colored like me.

That got my mind spinning, and I thought about Oklahoma City—remember what a jolt it was when it turned out to be an *American*—Tim McVeigh? We ask: how can "they" do things like this? Well—how could McVeigh blow up all those kids? How could an American do that?

We've heard a lot of people ask that question lately, about those pictures we really do wish we'd never seen, from the Iraq prison. "How could Americans do this?" I've even heard: "Americans *don't* do this." Well, Americans did, and we're just going to have to live with it. In the school curriculum wars, anyone still looking for a reason to include the stains in American history has one right here. Maybe we do have amnesia: our history is as shadowed as anyone's. (Senator Paul Simon, from Illinois, after sitting on the Senate Intelligence Committee and listening to the CIA, said that if anyone in the world came up to him and said "Your country did this awful thing," he wouldn't be able to deny it.)

I don't watch much television news, unless there's some crisis, but I tuned in Larry King—you know how he leans forward and gets that squinty look like a puzzled two-year-old who wonders why he can't go to the beach, and (I'm sure) I heard him ask his guest: "How could *human beings* do this?"

Human beings? Did he sleep through the 20th century? I wondered if he'd gone to high school.

When I was a freshman in boarding school, I once watched—wide-eyed in terror, hoping it wouldn't happen to me—about a dozen boys take one small boy and stuff him into his locker—we had these lockers for all the clothes we brought from home, everything we owned. They stuffed him in his locker, locked it (with his combination lock), took a can of lighter fluid, squirted some through the vent, and told him they were going to start dropping matches in unless he gave them his combination (so they could pillage his stuff at will).

A couple people shouted protests; one self-possessed person ran to get a priest to stop it.

But this was being done *for fun*. And these were children privileged and intelligent enough to be going to a private school—white, American Christians at a Christian school where we literally had church every day (yes, and twice on Sundays). A couple *were* malicious—I don't go to reunions, but I hope they've spent most of their lives in the caring hands of law enforcement—but most of them weren't. They were just carried along.

Human beings can come to a point where they're capable of almost anything—not all of us, but many of us. Take that locker room situation, make it not for fun but important and dangerous, put a veil of secrecy over it, and then tell them it's so urgent you've thrown away the rule book—where's the surprise? It's a moral catastrophe waiting to happen.

And now we approach from the dark side what we are about here. We all bear a divided nature. We confess year round in our brief order for public confession: "We are in bondage to sin and cannot free ourselves." Those aren't just empty words, something the gloomy Lutherans enjoy brooding on: they speak the fundamental truth about human nature and its need for redemption. They're not words for church—they're words for life: the life we live every day, the life we read about in the papers, the life and the choices we're propelled into when we find ourselves in a ghastly situation.

Why would we need the coming of Christ, and the gift of the Spirit, the call to see ourselves in the last days when we're in Christ, the call to enter the community of his name to be saved? Because we're in bondage to sin and cannot free ourselves.

I see Pentecost as the gift of the Spirit to a divided world, to people divided in themselves, from what they ought to be, something meant to gather in a new reality across those divisions, something for our healing and the healing of the nations.

I see it that way as the vision and the call of the gospel and I'd like to say we were that force.

I'd *like* to say it, but most days I don't think I can. On my worst days, I can get almost despairing about it. The Christian community is as divided and divisive as any other. Maybe that's just to remind us that we'll always need a miracle of the Spirit to get anywhere.

When I was at the seminary, we were talking about hymns once and one of the professors said he really loved an English hymn called "Jerusalem"—about Jesus walking on the green mountains and pleasant pastures of England—a truly ridiculous hymn, but they do sing it all the time: the professor said it was the English National Hymn and it was too bad we really didn't have a National Hymn.

So I said, "Oh, c'mon. We've got one—it's "The Battle Hymn of the Republic." Everybody knows it, and if you hear it anywhere, if you hear it played on a kazoo in Bulgaria, you'll think of the United States. We can all sing the chorus, it chokes us up, it's our hymn."

And he said, "No. It's a Northern hymn. Remember—it dates from the Civil War. I think half the country would disagree with you."

I thought about that conversation this week because I did pick it as a patriotic hymn and, to me, it does lift us to our best. But, yes, he's right—it does come from a divided time: the country wasn't just *divided*—we were *killing* EACH OTHER in vast, agonizing numbers: compared to Gettysburg and the Wilderness, the Iraq war would be a skirmish. And the Christian churches were divided with the country—if you've ever wondered why there are *Southern* Methodists and *Southern* Baptists, it was the war and slavery. Real divisions about real things—not to be just waved away: real divisions about values, people's lives and destinies, about "who is my neighbor?"

So let's call it a visionary hymn, because it is, and we sing it in hope: confessing our own sin and blindness, forcing ourselves to look for the coming of the Lord, a power not our own.

As you can probably tell, the pool of my memory was certainly stirred by the day—the *days* we're in. (But you can ask Mary Carol—I left out half the stories I was going to tell!!) But I did want to close with a quote from

Abraham Lincoln, the one about the "better angels of our nature." It's one of his nice meditations on reconciliation and I went looking for it in the 2nd Inaugural. But it was really from the *1st* Inaugural—with all the war, all the carnage, to come. But it's a good word for the day: it's a long speech and this is the last paragraph:

> I am loth to close. [Him, too!] We are not enemies, but friends. We must not be enemies. Though passion may have strained, it must not break our bonds of affection. The mystic chords of memory, stretching from every battlefield and patriot grave, to every living heart and hearthstone, all over this broad land, will yet swell the chorus of the Union, when again touched, as surely they will be, by the better angels of our nature.
>
> Amen.

2007

This sermon was given May 27, 2007. Once again, that Sunday was also the Feast of Pentecost, and the text for the sermon was Acts 2:1–21. Stories about the neglect and mistreatment of wounded troops had just been filling the media.

When I was a senior in high school, we were all having lunch one day in November, 1963, when one of the teachers called for silence to make an announcement: he told us that President John Kennedy had just been shot in Dallas. In the wake of that event, as we sat glued to the television whenever we could, I heard someone say for the first time: people alive today will remember where they were when they heard this news, the way older people remember the news about Pearl Harbor. I learned how an event can define a time, how an event can become a bond between people who have nothing else in common. "Where were you when you heard?" I think people already do that with the attack on the twin towers.

I remember where I was when Ronald Reagan was shot, too—though I wouldn't be sure everybody would. I was visiting a nursing home when I was on internship. I saw the news bulletin on one of the televisions, and I remember sagging against a doorway and feeling a wave of sorrow, even though I'd bet someone the American people couldn't possibly elect such a terrible actor to be president. But I especially remember the sorrow, because I did *not* remember feeling that sorrowful when President Kennedy was shot—but then, in 1981, I *was* older, I knew more about death, about pain and loss, I feared more social disorder and violence.

I remember, too, the first time I mentioned Pearl Harbor in a confirmation class and one of the students said: "What's that?" I realized I was beginning to outgrow the world. And part of the melancholy of aging is that the world really isn't yours anymore: fewer and fewer people around you have the same memories you do.

Many of us have known or will know that pain, that isolation, that exclusion, of personal memory loss: some of our older loved ones look at us in bewilderment and ask us who we are: it's a strange and lonely feeling. And how unimaginably frightening it must be to have the familiarity of the world vanish from around you. Shared memories are landmarks in time, they mark the contours of our lives, our experiences, our histories. They're just as vital for our lives in community: they bear not only our greater identities but our values, our ideals, our purposes. There's a moral dimension to memory: mothers and teachers and coaches and bosses all tell us: "Now when you're out there, *remember who you are*." And they don't think they have to say much else.

We come this weekend to one of our community landmarks—a day we actually name by memory: "Memorial Day"—where we proclaim our bond with the dead, our continuity and community with them. It's a day with ceremonies that call us to honor the dead of past wars, and *so honor* devotion and sacrifice, ideals that no community or family could *live* without. But because of the way death and the grave gather all in, turn our minds to the past and the reality and depth of sheer belonging, that basic claim: "these are *ours*," Memorial Day has become a kind of national Day of the Dead. People place flowers on the graves of all their loved ones, and who would tell them they had no place?

But for us gathered here, there is another landmark in time, another day that defines our identities and our values, our paths and purposes—the Day of Pentecost. There's always an interesting, and at this time especially appropriate, overlap between the church calendar and the national calendar. As long as Easter is celebrated on the first Sunday after the first full moon on or after March 21st, Memorial Day will often fall within or close to the season of Easter: the Christian facing of death and the promise of victory over the grave.

There was an English poet named Philip Larkin who wasn't himself a believer but he has a little poem where he talks about how much he likes to visit churches because they make him feel the past so strongly and how much the deep parts of our lives and our yearnings gather there—he says a church is 'a serious house on serious earth' and that people will always be drawn to churches when they feel a hunger for the seriousness of life, if only because churches gather in the dead and have such an evident bond with those who've died.

I think there is a truth there, and a truth we also feel when we're out at the cemetery in silence, on Memorial Day. The dead do root us in life, death gives a weight to our attachments.

That's a human truth, an important truth, but we who not only visit but *worship in* churches must speak a greater truth as well. We gather in the dead not because we're the house of death but because we're the house of life where the word of life is spoken: we have a bond with the dead because they live in Christ and we are one with them in the communion of saints. Whenever we dwell within serious and sober things, it's all the shadows that seem to take us and it's always important to be called back to where the real power is. Death and all it brings could have no power over us if life did not have our love. We feel loss because we feel love first. Death can bow us down: we will always need the word of life to lift us up, to remind us who we are.

I think there's a special anguish and grief upon us this Memorial Day. I don't think anyone can look at the conflict still going on without feeling anguish that our soldiers are still falling, still being wounded, being sent back again and again, four years on, with no one really seeing much light.

It's a time of anguish and regret.

I remember four years ago how hard it was to speak a word of caution, let alone of peace, without being ridiculed, shouted down, told you were a fool. I think there's a lot of regret; a lot of us would want the chance to listen back again.

I think there's a bitterness, too. Wasn't it hard to hear about the neglect of the wounded at Walter Reed hospital? What a bitter revelation. There's not an elected official in this country who didn't *proclaim* absolute and unqualified support for our troops—they're probably all out there doing it this weekend: and then to hear how neglected they are! Cast into squalor! To hear how the troubled are turned away! It's a bitter revelation and a national shame.

And it's a frightening time. It's frightening how much fury is loose in the world, how bad things could go, how many seeds might be sprouting of future horrors. It's easy to feel powerless and hopeless in a troubled world. Maybe it's easy to feel furious, too.

But we're not just spectators of life, and we're not its judges: we're participants. Everything we are and do contributes over time to the shape of all things. And we here are not just any participants—we're part of the body of Christ. As incredible as it may seem, as much as we want to forget it, as often as we have failed and will fail at it, Christians are actually supposed to do some good in the world—in this real, miserable world—or at least stand for something in it, hold out some hope for a better way.

So I want to turn to that other *day* we've come to, the Day of Pentecost, and take it as it was meant to be taken, as a defining moment of the church, the seed and image of what the church ideally is and is to be.

Anybody that knows anything about Pentecost knows it's the day the church as a community sort of lurched into being through being visited by the Holy Spirit, in wind and fire. *So*: we often think about Pentecost as a moment of *excitement, motivation, zeal*. Christian groups that describe themselves as *Pentecostal* strive for excitement and emotion. We say church events are spirit-filled when they're exciting. We poor old Lutherans are often chastised by our more antic brethren as being bereft of Spirit.

But all of that is what you settle for when you've given up on what you're supposed to be.

Acts says the disciples were filled with the Holy Spirit—but it doesn't go on to say they were excited, but that they spoke in other languages. People aren't amazed at their emotional outburst: people are amazed because they *understand them.*

Pentecost isn't a miracle of excitement, but a miracle of *understanding*. It's about crossing the boundaries of nations and the confusions of languages with the one clear word of the gospel. It's about shattering the boundaries that keep tribes apart. It's about *healing the divisions of nations*, divisions embodied in our very speech. Pentecost presents the church, the community of faith, *us*, as a new force on earth, a new difference-making reality, a new people that will heal the divisions and the strife of the earth by calling people beyond their natural communities of blood, soil, race, clan, into the community of Christ, the faith community, of the Spirit.

This can't be stressed too much: a lot of the good we're supposed to do on earth involves the healing of divisions, deep divisions. The Bible portrays languages as a mark of human division and, after the Tower of Babel, a punishment for human arrogance. Crossing at Pentecost that divide of languages is thus a sign of promise and healing: it's a purpose of the church—to find a way into everyone's heart, to call them to Christ, to heal the nations—the strife between nations—by being a reality greater than they are. That's what amazes the crowd at Pentecost: that a word has come **to** *them*: they didn't have to learn Latin or Hebrew—the word came to them, as Jesus came to earth. 'How is it that we hear, each of us, in our own native language?'

But look how easily the catalog of nations trips off their tongues! That's the world they know. They are comfortable with those divisions—comfortable with the world's strife. And they hear what really is the promise in that word but they hear it as a judgment: *each* in our own language—*our own*: it's come to me, I'm on the spot, *I* have to hear: but also *each*: it's *for* all—there's nothing special about me. Pentecost puts the nations in their place.

We've kept faith with part of that: we have *gone into* all the nations of the earth—sometimes the first dictionaries written in a language will be written by Christian missionaries.

But the boundaries of the earth are still pretty strong: and our failure to heal the nations can be read around the world in the military cemeteries of nations that are broadly Christian.

Our own local cemetery, the G.A.R. cemetery—from "The Grand Army of the Republic," dates from after the Civil War: when our nation fought out whether it would remain one or become two nations. But it was Christian against Christian. In one of Lincoln's famous speeches, the 2nd Inaugural Address, he was summing up the Civil War: "Both [sides] read the same Bible, and pray to the same God; and each invokes His aid against the other." Christian against Christian—but the Christian bond was weaker than the bonds of region, custom, family, state; the Christian word was claimed and swallowed up by those, put in service of those lesser bonds.

It happens easily enough. We belong to those natural communities, and sometimes everything in our hearts pulls us into conflict. The last hymn we'll sing today is "The Battle Hymn of the Republic"—it's both a

Christian song and a war song, a *Northern* song, and 150 years later I still can't say both sides were the same or that the war wasn't worth fighting. I suppose that means I'm as sinful as everybody else.

Our church—the Lutheran church—has never been completely a peace church: Lutheran moral thought has always recognized that, on a sinful earth, force, warfare, might be a necessary evil: that sometimes, on a sinful earth, there is no other way to do any good that could be done.

I believe that, but I also believe most of the time there is another way. Most of the time there is.

The followers of the Prince of Peace should be the ones looking for that other way. We should not be the first to cry out for conflict. The world never lacks for the cheerleaders of war, who think it will be so easy, so easily controlled. What the world needs most are voices that will speak peace, hands that will find the ways to peace.

We here have a bond, every Christian around the world has a bond, to those first believers called out to be the healing of the nations. We should all remember, more often than we do, who we are.

Amen.

2008

This sermon, given on May 25, 2008, is a revised version of the sermon I gave two years earlier on Memorial Day Weekend, May 28, 2006. It's an oddity in this collection since it was preached in a different parish than the others. My wife Mary Carol and I, who served as co-pastors, had been asked to act as interim ministers in a neighboring church that was waiting for a new pastor. It was a busy time. I revised a lot of old sermons to use there and often found myself, as with this one, preferring the revision. What makes this revision even a bit odder is that I was using a different gospel reading: the 2006 version was given on the seventh Sunday of Easter, and the gospel was John 17:6–19; I also used the story about choosing new witnesses from Acts 1:15–17, 21–26; the 2008 version, because Easter was quite early that year, was given on the second Sunday after Pentecost, when the gospel was Matthew 6:24–34. It was, in any case, Memorial Day itself rather than the readings that had been driving my meditation in 2006, and I found it challenging and interesting to set my reflections on the Day against a different moment of the gospel story. I also found it interesting that I didn't feel the need to change much in those reflections. The question I raise towards the end—"How many Memorial Days is this since these gnawing, unresolvable wars began?"—was even more pointed with two more years gone by.

This sermon reveals another reality of parish life: the effect of fatigue. With the extra travel—our two churches were sixty miles apart—and the extra funerals, meetings, visits, and classes, I reached a point, too many weeks, when I was worn out by Saturday and my ability to concentrate was eroding. As I was finishing this sermon, I couldn't find my way to an ending, and simply stole a few words and thoughts from yet another Memorial Day sermon, from 2007, the preceding sermon printed here.

I was putting away a DVD the other day when my fingers trailed fondly across a movie that I realized I hadn't watched since I bought it but that—obviously—I liked well enough to buy: it was called *V for Vendetta* and it was a weirdly moving, futuristic thriller about a terrorist revenge plot in a London of the future, but it got its force by stirring the contemporary stew of fear and terrorism, power and rage, plots and suspicion and popular discontent that we're all bubbling in. But it jumped out at me because, with Memorial Day coming up, I *remembered* it began with a call to *memory*: right at the beginning there was a voiceover, a young woman's hushed voice saying:

> Remember, remember,
> The fifth of November.

Now, do *you* remember the fifth of November? Some of us probably do, and "London" would be the giveaway: November 5th is Guy Fawkes Day in England and what you're supposed to remember is the foiling of the infamous gunpowder plot of 1605: a group of Roman Catholic conspirators—today we'd call them "fundamentalist extremists"or "Christian terrorists"—felt they were being strangled by the penal laws against Roman Catholics and decided to send a message to the true-hearted Protestant English government on the opening day of Parliament by filling the cellar of the House of Lords with 36 barrels of gunpowder overlaid with iron bars and firewood, and blowing up King James I (of Bible fame) along with the Lords and the Commons. The plot was uncovered, Fawkes was arrested in the cellar, and they're still burning Guy Fawkes in effigy, 400 years on.

Say you know all that. You hear that little rhyme—"Remember, remember, the fifth of November"—and you *do* recognize that it's a kind of moral summons to affirm an identity—*but* it doesn't pull your heart because it's not *your* identity. You realize another community organizes its fears and its loyalties around a different event (that really doesn't touch us).

But now suppose I said: *remember* with me a day in *September*—call to your mind the bloodiest single day in American history: I would guess, for most Americans today, both the identity and the emotion would rise immediately: we would say we remember September 11, 2001: we know it as ours and we feel its impact.

I say: I think most Americans would say that but we'd actually be wrong about the identity of the date: in fact, September 11 is not the bloodiest single day in American history. That day is (still) September 17, 1862, the battle of Antietam. About 6,400 Union and Confederate soldiers died in the battle or shortly after. (To make a vivid comparison, the first county I served in as a pastor had a population of about 5,000.)

Another 15,000 were wounded, many seriously maimed. (Those numbers are double or more of September 11.) They're four times more than American casualties at Normandy on June 6, 1944.

Those are staggering losses, with unimaginable effects on the communities those soldiers came from. (Look at the anguish we're going through from Iraq.) And that was one day in a four-year war. (I guess, when you think about it, memory has a lot to do with sorrow and grief.)

Any story of the Civil War pulls our hearts more than the story of Guy Fawkes, and it has nothing to do with magnitude of loss. September 11, 2001, will stir *us* more deeply than either the Gunpowder Plot *or* Antietam. I don't have to *tell* you that: you *feel* it as I name the events. It has to do with immediacy, how we sense our involvement.

Memory is local: it lives on particular faces, particular names, particular events that are dear to us, close to us, part of us, that fill out our world when we wake up every morning.

Memory's a living thing—and it's a human thing: it can be mistaken, or misled, or misused. The governments of the modern age have worked hard to distort it, and they're still working hard. (The great struggle in Gorge Orwell's *1984* is about memory, controlling it, correcting it.)

Memory can expand, or contract. We can, for many reasons, forget.

One reason the Civil War is *worth* remembering is that's the war Memorial Day dates from. One of the people involved in starting Memorial Day was a Union general born in Pastor Mary Carol's hometown—Murphysboro, Illinois (if you'd like another local connection): General John A. Logan. (I've seen his statue there—it's the smallest state park in

Illinois. There's a better one in Grant Park in Chicago.) One year at the Memorial Day ceremonies, one of the speakers said Logan fought for the Confederacy and I thought Mary Carol was going to have a stroke. She comes from the southern tip of Illinois, and you can still start a pretty vicious fight down there with a Confederate flag—they don't consider it a cute decoration. (Another reason the Civil War's worth remembering is that it's not over yet.)

But Memorial Day's always a moving day. And the most moving thing about it is what's most characteristic about it: think of our holidays: at Christmas, we exchange gifts, gather around Christmas trees, sing the carols, and light candles; Fourth of July we eat hot dogs and watch fireworks; Thanksgiving we *just* eat, I guess—it's a very focused kind of festival; on Memorial Day, we go out to the cemetery and stand among the dead, beside the graves of our community's past. (Especially veterans—but because of that leveling reality of death, we gather all the dead to us.) That's a striking act.

There's nothing more humbling or enlarging than standing beside a grave. You feel less important but more connected. Memory gains weight and force: there's a broadening of life and community, a reaching out for a unity that transcends time.

I've often thought it's hard to do anything in a cemetery that doesn't seem like an act of worship. You may go there thinking only of human connections but it's hard not to see you're before larger forces that enclose human life.

So there's a kind of spiritual convergence between the founding *impulse* and the *act* of Memorial Day and what we are about (constantly) as a religious community. We bow before the larger forces that enclose human life, and we name their source and their goal in the God who created and redeemed us. We—as a believing community—only exist through the bonds of memory. And part of *our* local identity, what pulls our hearts and has a claim on our heart's direction is the call of Jesus and his gathering of disciples, his giving them—giving us—an identity and a purpose: to be a new force.

Today's gospel reading is the passage where I think Jesus sounds most like a hippie. I'm showing my age but, reading it, I find myself singing a Kris Kristofferson song from back in the day called "Jesus was a Capricorn," where Kris points out that Jesus ate organic food, didn't wear shoes, believed in peace, and had long hair. Partly it's the imagery—birds, flowers, grass; more deeply, it's the apparent lack of effort or concern —"don't worry about tomorrow."

Jesus is siding with the grasshoppers against the ants.

But it's the deepest part of all that makes the difference: he's calling us from faith in ourselves, faith in our own gain (which has no end), the path of our own satisfactions—from those, to faith in God, service in God's kingdom.

He's giving us teachings but the gospel bears those teachings to us within the story of his life: *he's* the event we believers organize our fears and loyalties around. He teaches us to *fear* things the world *trusts*: like wealth and power. Our constant return to Jesus is an act of memory we almost don't notice—but this passage is a good example of its necessity:

left to ourselves, we would teach and live nothing like this: in fact, quite the opposite.

But the church never doubted the importance of memory: there's a wonderful passage in our first reading that touches on our *fear* of being *forgotten* and sees God's compassion as borne by memory:

> "Thus says the Lord:...Can a woman forget her nursing child, or show no compassion for the child of her womb? Even these may forget yet, I will not forget you. See, I have inscribed you on the palms of my hands." (Isaiah 49:8a, 15–16)

Wonderful, powerful image.

But let's step back and consider: faith depends on remembering that. *Somebody* has to remember it. In 1 Corinthians, Paul says: "Think of us in this way, as...stewards of God's mysteries." The caretakers, the keepers of the truths about God, the keepers of the memory of faith. What's especially poignant about that claim of Paul's, to be a servant of Christ and a steward of God's mysteries, is that he wasn't a living witness to Jesus' time on earth, a physical witness to the actual events. He was passing on a faith he came late to, and you can follow a worry through the New Testament witnesses: Who will keep the faith when we are gone?

That reminded me of when I was very small: around Memorial Day, the *Chicago Tribune* would interview the dwindling handful of still-living veterans of the Civil War, these sturdy old coots, about 100 plus years old. (I remember one of them was asked what he attributed his long life to, and he said, "Well, sir, I guess I'd have to say: moonshine and chewin' tobaccy.")

Precious witnesses, but all gone now. And we're all children of time, we'll all pass away in time.

Memory has to travel. *What* is remembered, *what* story is told becomes vitally important, once no one can say "But I was there." Every act of teaching is a charge to memory.

The hearts of disciples have to rise in faith to claim a part in those stories. And as time passes, those are the only witnesses there are. We are now the stewards of God's mysteries, witnesses through the memories we've received.

That's as much gift as responsibility. What our hearts rise to embrace are the very things that become its treasures, the things that make us who we are.

One of the great novels of World War II is a Russian novel called *Life and Fate*. It's roughly set around the battle of Stalingrad, but it tours a lot of Soviet society and it's been said it's the one novel that makes you feel what it was like to live under Stalin's regime.

The author's name was Vassily Grossman, and he was a Jew. And when the German army invaded the Soviet Union, their advance was so fast they overran the village Grossman's mother lived in before he could get her out—and, of course, the Germans deported and gassed Russian Jews as they did all other Jews. Grossman never forgave himself.

In his novel, as a witness to that time, Grossman tried to imagine what it was like for his mother and others from his village to go to the gas chamber. The part that moved me the most was that he didn't overwhelm you with numbers or dwell so much on the humiliation and the pain as talk about the preciousness and uniqueness of each person's *memory*. One woman remembers watching geese in a meadow, reading *Huckleberry Finn*, looking at the stars, picking tomatoes out of a market bin—and he describes that flame of memory dying out as the gas comes upon her. Then your mind moves to how many died, and it really is overwhelming.

Let's go back to what Jesus says in the gospel, with all the cruelty and the sorrow of the earth in mind. When he says, "I tell you, do not worry about your life… do not worry about tomorrow," you can't believe he's being serious—especially if you come to the words with human misery in mind.

But look: he begins by considering what masters your life, what you give your soul to, what you see in life. The lightness, the airiness, the apparent frivolousness of his images—the birds of the air, the lilies of the field—are picked because they *don't* amount to much and they *can't* do much. That highlights how dependent they are on greater forces. Jesus is pushing one of his extreme points: they endure *anyway*, gloriously, beautifully. The providence of God watches over them. He's making us think about what it would be like to be that powerless: see—God would sustain you. And anyway: Just how powerful are you?

Strive for the kingdom of God: leave what you think you need to God. He's *reminding* us of God's providence, calling us to turn from our desperate wanting, and *calling* us to rise to hope with a kind of purity: hope in a power not our own, hope when we know not what to hope for.

It's not a bad thing to be reminded of and called to, especially in a cruel and sorrowful world.

The last few years, as Memorial Day approached, I've found myself wondering: how many Memorial Days is this since these gnawing, unresolvable wars we're in began, the wars we went off to so confidently? How many of us thought our troops would still be there, in an anguishing situation, that we'd still be mourning the newly fallen, three, four, five Memorial Days down the road?

It's hard not to remember some of the easy optimism there was. Remember how the Iraq war was going to be a cakewalk? But I don't mean just the politicians: someone remarked to me when I was sitting in the dentist's office, "Oh, why don't we just attack and get it over with?" (Yeah. Let's get it over with.) As though sending young men and women out to die and be maimed were nothing, as though subjecting civilians to these horrific weapons were nothing.

I remember how hard it was five years ago to speak a word of caution, let alone a word of peace. It's so easy to forget how uncontrollable war is.

We should renew each Memorial Day our memory of what wars cost, how much devastation they bring. We don't all pay that cost, and we owe honor and reverence to those who did *and still do*. But we shouldn't just honor them after they pay it, but before they have to, by looking to our responsibilities, to do what we can to heal the hostilities of the world.

And we especially, we who hear the call of Jesus to walk a different path, we followers of the Prince of Peace, should find ways to bring his light to the world, ways to cross its divisions. We shouldn't be the first to cry out for conflict. The world never lacks for the cheerleaders of war. What the world needs most are voices that will speak peace, hands that will find the way to peace. Hope in God's kingdom can be a power against the fears of the earth.

We stewards of God's mysteries have a bond to those first witnesses called out to be a new people, a new force on earth, servants of Christ. May we remember who we are most deeply. And may we all find, by his light, a way from the fury of the earth to the peace of the kingdom of God.

Amen.

2009

This sermon was given May 24, 2009. It was the seventh Sunday of Easter and the gospel reading was John 17:6–19. It was also the Sunday we honored our graduates.

A couple of years ago, some of us who'd been at the seminary together were talking about our changing attitudes toward our birthdays: one person claimed he never remembered it, some had things they always did, but one woman said: "I can't think of my birthday anymore without feeling terrible."

So we laughed, started teasing her about fearing old age, and she said: "You guys don't know when my birthday is, do you?"

No.

"It's September 11th."

Oh.

This *was* a couple of years ago, and maybe there wouldn't be the same instant comprehension now; maybe there would.

What would we say had happened, though? That a greater event had pushed her aside? That someone else's purpose had swallowed her up?

That she was forced to awaken, as most of us are not, from the dream that our private reality is secure and absolutely important?

But then we would have to say: there are far worse ways of that happening to you.

I think, at the time, I said something like: there's probably a horrible occurrence on every date in the world's calendar—we're just not aware of it; in fact, it's likely someone is suffering horribly somewhere on earth every moment we live. Well, that cheered everybody up—but there are a lot of avenues you can follow from that reflection: how ignorant we usually are (and maybe want to be); how vulnerable life really is (and we never know how much); and how every birthday, milestone, celebration, blessing we live to enjoy really is worth giving thanks for.

The world and the people in it don't order their ways for our benefit. That's probably the first shock of learning we get, when someone much bigger than us says no, or "not now"—and it's a little puzzling that it continues to be such a shock. But what our life is, who we are, is not completely in our power, what marks us as the people we are in the time we live in.

That being so, once again: every milestone, celebration, blessing, we come to really is worth giving thanks for, a confluence of effort, achievement, protection, prevention, nutrition, good weather, social stability, employment, antibiotics, and dumb luck almost as amazing as the appearance of life on the third planet from the sun and nowhere else, as far as we know.

Today, at Faith, we celebrate one of those milestones: we honor the young people of our faith community who are graduating this year; we congratulate you for your efforts; and we give thanks for everyone and everything that helped bring you to this day.

But I got to thinking about the many layers that make up our lives, the things beyond our control that mark us, because this is also Memorial Day weekend, a day we also have honored here, and taken as an occasion of thanksgiving.

When you think about it, most graduations do occur somewhere near Memorial Day, but my guess is we often act as though those ceremonies are happening in different worlds. Depending on who's in this year's graduating class, you might or might not see a completely different crowd at the school and at the cemetery.

But Graduation Day and Memorial Day would always have something to say to each other: it's good to recall on Graduation Day just how hard the world is, how costly life can get; good to recall on Memorial Day just how young the dead can be.

And, at a deeper level, schools and cemeteries, learning and burying, are deep and vital parts of any community's life. They're part of our fight against the dark, the way we order our passage through time, carry within us and witness to where we've come from, who we are, what we value, what we want to keep and hand on.

In a town like ours, the church, the school, and the cemeteries are all within walking distance of each other. You can stroll down our hall and see young smiling faces that you can see slightly older versions of on the walls of the school, and then go read their names on gravestones. In a half-day's walk, you can trace a century's passing.

But we only have the ceremonies we do because we live in time, and *because we remember*—the human gift of memory allows us to live not for a day, but *with* the generations before us and *for* the generations after us.

This year's graduates might gaze out at the miserable, multidimensional mess the world's in and conclude that the last couple of generations could have done a little better job at this. I'd have to agree: in one of my notes for this sermon, I wondered if I should apologize on behalf of all the old fools—I also noted: "we pass along not only our knowledge but our debts, and the unintended consequences of our brilliant decisions."

Across the country tomorrow, we'll be honoring the graves of young people who didn't graduate that long ago, and who were maybe just looking to learn a trade or pay for college, but had to bear the burden. We'll be honoring people like that next year and more—from two wars nobody thought would last this long: but everybody, *everybody*, should have known at the start that they *could*. That's a good thing to *remember* the next time somebody tells us how easy, how quick, how cheap war can be.

It *is* an anxious and a troubled world. Still, I believe it's always, always, better to *know* that than to imagine otherwise. The graduates of 2009 probably have a more accurate picture of the world than the graduates of 1959, raised on Eisenhower, Howdy Doody, Ozzie and Harriet, Wonder Bread, and gasoline that cost less than 25 cents a gallon.

Moreover, once we've said the worst about *our* time, we haven't even come close to saying the worst about what the world has been at other times, and *could* be in the future. And if we could take the time to say all that, we still would not have said what's most important.

We're sitting in a building in one small town in Minnesota, USA. But, in this building, we sit before God, we sit under the cross of Christ. In this place, when we've said the worst there is to say about the world and human sin, we haven't even begun to speak.

In this place, this day, there is one more dimension to our celebration beyond honoring our graduates and remembering our dead: we call this Sunday, a bit ploddingly, the Seventh Sunday of Easter, and it's something we don't think about that much—but we're inside our community's time of rejoicing in Christ's victory: *redemption* from death, and a *summons* to life, promise, and call to us as Christian disciples. One more dimension to our lives: in time, but beyond it, too: the same promise and call that has gone out to every Christian, in every time and place. No matter how the world looks and is, we are called to love God, love neighbor, and follow the way of the cross in service and sacrifice. *That* we can do anytime, anyplace, anywhere.

Let me make you feel better yet: as Jesus says, wealth and power would only make that harder to do!

The passage I read from John's gospel could almost be called the first disciples' graduation address; it's the last, long thing Jesus says to the disciples, his long goodbye, as though he were trying to pour a lifetime of instruction into one farewell lecture—and Jesus wasn't the last teacher or parent to try to do that.

When you hear this read, it seems like he's talking in circles—this is only a small part, but the more you hear, the more you feel like that. In fact, when you study New Testament Greek, it's John's writings that you read first because you don't need much of a vocabulary: if you have these words—God, world, you, me, love, joy, truth—you'll get a lot of it.

Those perceptions of how it sounds are on the right track to seeing and feeling what Jesus really is saying. He seems to talk in circles because this faith is a kind of circle: a circle of life: he in us, we in God, God in him, life flowing through us and among us, once we've been gathered in.

The voice of Jesus that the Gospel of John lets you hear is very serene, very peaceful, and that's a power in itself, qualities faith can bring us to share. But it *can* be a little hard to see what he's talking about because he's speaking way above the details—in a couple of ways.

First, he's not mentioning the hard realities of *his* world, similar to the ones I began by talking about in ours: but Judas has just walked out to betray him; he knows he's about to be arrested and tortured to death; that's going to happen on a cross because *his* country is under foreign occupation and that's how the Romans teach people to behave; and some scholars think Jesus was so attuned to the dangers of wealth because the community he grew up in was being squeezed economically.

He had to live with the troubles we do; he didn't let them define him.

Second, more importantly, he's speaking above the details of faith itself, the little rules, the do's and don'ts that mean so much to us but have no life in them. He's presenting the breadth and depth of faith, faith as a way of living that breaks down walls, that moves toward unity, that lives out of and within love, a faith that is a force of God in the world *that way*.

That's the calling of every Christian Disciple: to live out a faith that's a force of God in the world like that.

It's a calling deeper than our vocations, a calling we can follow within all our different vocations. We can follow it in the greatest or the smallest arena, and it will always have the same value in the sight of God. It's not about power, wealth, fame—all the sicknesses that are rotting us—our arrogance, our desperate grasping: those are things the gospel *saves us from*. Those are things the servants of the gospel help heal in the world.

One of the things that always amazes me in the gospel and the stories of the first disciples is that while Jesus and his followers are clearly filled with purpose they manage to find that purpose in whatever comes along, no matter how derailed they seem to be. They keep getting shipwrecked, jailed, exiled, detoured—and I think what's behind that sense of unwavering purpose is their seeing anything and everything as a matter of faithfulness in the sight of God. They have a core of peace within them: what *they* want, what *they* plan is not important: faithful witness, *whatever happens*, is important.

Let me close by tracing another side of this gospel passage:

It's striking that Jesus is both praying and teaching (or teaching by praying), that he's talking to God and the disciples (as well as to us, *through* the disciples)—reminding God that his disciples are continuing his mission, and are probably going to need help, reminding the rest of us that, *as* his disciples, we have a life to live up to, an identity to be maintained—the truth of his word—and that maintaining that won't happen by itself.

We're called to that life in an anxious and troubled world. But it's also a world that, to the eyes of faith, is lit by the dawn of Easter. We're called to live in Easter's light. The risen Christ makes all the things of the earth, its fearful shadows, its delusions and intoxications, seem small. He brings healing to the earth's divisions and its wounds.

All the world needs his touch, in its despair, in its vanity, in its injustice, in its pain. The world needs the witness of all the ordinary followers of Christ.

May we all find, by his light, a way through the trouble of the earth to the peace of the kingdom of God.

Amen.

IV. JUDGEMENT

The conflict between Christianity and the state will become particularly apparent in times of war; but it will not be perfectly understood if it is not anticipated in other than martial periods....Nowhere is the temptation to idolatry greater than in national life.

    —Reinhold Niebuhr, "Four Hundred to One,"
      Beyond Tragedy

I

Reading them now, I am struck most by how timid these sermons seem, how often they rush into harmless theological reflection.

I remember stepping into the pulpit, sometimes gasping from nervous apprehension, hoping I wouldn't hyperventilate, hoping my voice wouldn't quaver or rise an octave or disappear entirely, hoping I wouldn't choke up, from either bitterness or emotional idealism. There were passages I couldn't read aloud the night before without shaking with emotion, and I read them over and over to blunt their force for myself so I might deliver them effectively.

I remember them as edgier, riskier. Though they were of that time, they no longer bring back that time to me. Or perhaps they help reveal it. The timidity and the theological camouflage came from having to speak them to people I lived and worked with, many of whom thought otherwise than I did, some of them violently otherwise.

The parts that seem liveliest to me now are the discussions of war, the realities of past wars, the testimony of witnesses. But, once again, my memory betrays me: I had remembered this material as more extensive, as coming closer to the ends of the sermons than to the beginnings, more climactic. Perhaps to me it was, perhaps once I presented what I thought was edgy and challenging I turned with relief to things more comfortable and familiar.

I'm also surprised at the amount of indirection, speaking of present wars through past wars, speaking of my son or my daughter, using my experiences or my own lapses as indirect challenges. I'm surprised at some of the humor, at some of the easy targeting of politicians. Some of these things might be claimed as strategies of communication; I know some of them were strategies of self-protection.

Anyone who heard me wildly rant about the war in private would probably have been surprised at how guarded my words were in the pulpit.

I would often say, to those I trusted, that I thought Bush, Cheney, and Rumsfeld should be brought to trial—for criminal incompetence, if nothing else—and sentenced to emptying bed pans in VA hospitals for the rest of their lives, or that they should be turned over to the International Court to be tried as war criminals. After the American torture and abuse of prisoners was revealed, and long after it became clear the Iraq war was begun on false pretenses, I would point out that, after World War II, the United States and its allies had *executed* German and Japanese leaders for much the same things our own had done and were doing. When I heard conservatives describe America as a "moral," let alone a "Christian," nation or heard the Republican party referred to as the "party of responsibility," I would rage that such statements were grotesque so long as people like Bush, Cheney, and Rumsfeld were allowed to live in comfortable retirement.

But I never came close to saying anything like this in the pulpit. I could question how much good this would have done. I could question further if I ought not to have done it anyway.

I might say—and I would be speaking truthfully—that I would always try to be sensitive to the privilege I had in having a pulpit, that I didn't want to abuse that privilege, that I wanted always to speak fairly and within the limits of my calling. I might also say, truthfully, that I was very aware that fear of offending my community could have a hidden force beyond my ability to measure honestly.

I can still wonder if I would be happier with myself if I had shouted my most extreme judgements in my sermons.

And yet here's one more truthful statement: I honestly can't imagine myself doing that.

I'm not sure that I could unravel why I can't.

II

In the main entrance hall of the church I am a member of now, in retirement, there is a framed list of the young people in the congregation currently serving in the armed forces. It's a quiet testimony of honor and concern. It's not an occasional or seasonal display, like harvest decorations or hearts for St. Valentine's Day: it's always there, and no one would think of questioning its presence. In many of the churches I visit, there are similar displays. No one has any trouble understanding why they're there.

The ease of understanding is revealing.

When I was struggling with the Vietnam War and pacifism, I studied a lot of material about peace and war in church history, and I came across some things revealing in a different way, by their strangeness. I used to give, early in my service, a little course on Christian views of war and peace and every group I spoke to was bewildered by these things: one was a remark by Basil the Great in the fourth century that, even though killing in war was different than murder, those who had shed blood should abstain from communion *for three years*; the other was a decision by a council of bishops, after the Norman conquest of England, requiring penance for killing in war—one year for killing, forty days if you weren't sure the wound you had given had been fatal, and, if you didn't know how many you'd killed, one day a week *for the rest of your life.* (Those are taken from Roland Bainton's *Christian Attitudes toward War and Peace.*)

Note that the abstention from communion and the penances are not given to those who've killed *dishonorably* in *unjust* wars. They're not punishments for bad people who've committed atrocities. They are serious healing rituals for shedding blood in any war at all, for the guilt of war itself.

It's almost impossible to imagine things like this being required in an American Christian church today. For most of us, such demands are almost incomprehensible. Last Veterans' Day, my church asked veterans to stand: they were applauded and thanked for their service. Again, it is impossible for me to conceive of anyone suggesting they be barred from communion.

But if we consider the terrible memories of war settling within and burdening the lives of veterans, the suicides among both veterans and serving personnel, whatever it was that made my father sit on my bed and relive the war, we might ask which church takes the moral reality of war and the experience of war more seriously: the church that acknowledges the horror of killing and its harm to the spirit by demanding penance or the church that offers applause? We might ask: which takes its own mission more seriously? It's screamingly obvious a church like Basil's understood itself as, essentially and necessarily, a force for peace.

It's obvious we don't.

Every church I know prays for the men and women of the armed forces; few denounce the wars, the imperial policies and the blind faith in violence that send them around the world. We helplessly accept the deadly realities of human power. We hardly notice we've become its chaplains, if not its cheerleaders. It hardly occurs to us we might be something else.

III

In the fall of 2013, the conference pastors' group I meet with sponsored a day-long presentation on preaching in Advent and Christmas. The speaker was interesting enough, and sometimes provocative enough, and it was a pleasant enough day. Since I'm retired, I don't have regular preaching duties, but it's nice to be part of this group of thoughtful, compassionate pastors. It helps, in the America of today, that we're all fairly liberal politically: we're spared those awkward moments at ministerial brunches when the wrong issue comes up in the wrong group.

Anyway, towards the end of the afternoon, the speaker touched on the gospel for the Feast of the Holy Innocents, Martyrs: Matthew's story of Herod's massacre of the babies at Bethlehem. He paused for a moment to reflect on violence in the world and he said this:

"We Lutherans aren't one of the pacifist churches. We recognize that in a sinful world force is sometimes needed to help our neighbor, to protect our neighbor. And that God is at work then, too. Luther speaks of Two Kingdoms: the Kingdom of the Right Hand and the Kingdom of the Left Hand."

He held up his two hands, smiling, and stepped to the side of the podium. "Two hands. The hand of mercy and forgiveness, grace: the hand that will save us. The hand of force and punishment: the hand that must be used sometimes in a sinful world. We acknowledge that."

He smiled and shook his head. "But we don't go out and slaughter innocent people just because we want to kill one person. All so we can maintain ourselves in power."

He returned to the podium and his lecture. No one responded to his remark.

This was the fall of 2013. I wondered if he'd read any newspapers in the last twelve years. For all that time, "we," America, had been slaughtering innocent people around the world because we were after one man, then another man, then another, who we thought threatened our power. In Iraq and Afghanistan, we slaughtered and maimed more innocents that got in our way than Herod *could* have slaughtered in Bethlehem, with weapons Herod couldn't have imagined. "We" think nothing of sending our missiles and drones against neighborhoods, wedding parties, funeral gatherings, taxi drivers, and gardeners if we think they might also kill the one or two or several people we are after at the time.

I take that speaker's offhand, self-satisfied judgement and the unprotesting silence that followed it—our silence—as a damning measure of the moral blindness infecting American Christians.

"You are the salt of the earth; but if salt has lost its taste, how can its saltiness be restored? It is no longer good for anything…" (Matthew 5:13)

www.ingramcontent.com/pod-product-compliance
Lightning Source LLC
Chambersburg PA
CBHW080518090426
42734CB00015B/3101